Praise for OFF TO SAVE THE WORLD

"Julia Taft was one of a kind. Ann Blackman has captured this extraordinary woman with a passion that equals her passionate personality. She brought a voice, a commitment and tireless purpose to our cause, making US NGOs a force to be reckoned with in policy circles."
—WILLIAM S. REESE, *President and CEO, International Youth Foundation*

"Everyone who knew Julia Taft has a favorite 'Julia story' and *Off to Save the World* is a treasure chest of stories about an incredible individual whose passion, wit, and charm empowered people impacted by disasters worldwide. I had the privilege to work with and learn from Julia and will be using the chapters detailing Julia's involvement with Operation Lifeline Sudan, the Armenian Earthquake, the War in Bosnia, etc., as case studies that illuminate the qualities of leaders in the humanitarian field for our students in the Master of Science in Disaster Resilience Leadership program at Tulane University."
—KY LUU, *Executive Director,*
Disaster Resilience Leadership Academy, Tulane University

"Julia Taft was a consummate humanitarian whose intelligence, openness, and deep caring for the world's most vulnerable people will continue to be sorely missed. Ann Blackman has written a highly entertaining and very enlightening book about Julia's unusually productive life. We need more books like this and more people like Julia Taft."
—RON WALDMAN, *Founding Director, Program on Forced Migration and Health,* Mailman School of Public Health, Columbia University

OFF TO SAVE THE WORLD

How JULIA TAFT *Made a Difference*

ANN BLACKMAN

OFF TO SAVE THE WORLD
How Julia Taft Made a Difference

©2011 Ann Blackman

ISBN: 978-1-936447-55-8

Set in Minion Pro
Designed by David Allen
Manufactured in the United States of America

Printed by Maine Authors Publishing
558 Main Street, Rockland, Maine 04841
www.maineauthorspublishing.com

Cover photo
The Dalai Lama leaving the U.S. State Department with Julia Taft.
By Shawn Thew, AFP/Getty Images.

DEDICATION

In memory of Julia, a cherished friend,

and

For her children, Maria, William and Julie, with my love,

and, at Julia's request,

For her friends in the field.

To Carol & Peter,

With lots of love

Julie & Christo?

To laugh often and much;
To win the respect of intelligent people and the affection of children;
To appreciate beauty, to find the best in others;
To leave the world a bit better, whether by a healthy child, a garden patch
Or a redeemed social condition;
To know even one life has breathed easier because you have lived.
This is to have succeeded.

—RALPH WALDO EMERSON

TABLE OF CONTENTS

PREFACE 3

Chapter 1 BEGINNINGS. 23

Chapter 2 THE CIA: A SPY IS NOT BORN 29

Chapter 3 THE WHITE HOUSE FELLOWS. 33

Chapter 4 LOVE, WATERGATE & HEW 47

Chapter 5 INDOCHINESE REFUGEE RESETTLEMENT . . . 53

Chapter 6 AQUARIUS. 61

Chapter 7 OPERATION LIFELINE SUDAN 69

Chapter 8 THE ARMENIAN EARTHQUAKE 77

Chapter 9 WAR IN BOSNIA: 1992-1995 91

Chapter 10 INTERACTION: "HERDING CATS" 99

Chapter 11 REFUGEE CRISIS IN KOSOVO 105

Chapter 12 THE UNITED NATIONS: AFGHANISTAN. . . . 115

Chapter 13 JULIA & THE DALAI LAMA:
           A SPIRITUAL JOURNEY. 121

           ACKNOWLEDGMENTS 129

           ENDNOTES 131

           ABOUT THE BOOK 137

PREFACE

Her husband, Will, said it best in saying good-bye.

"One picture: Julia is leaving for work in the morning. Hanging about her is a pocketbook that is never completely closed, a Kenyan bag crammed full of e-mails and papers, and a briefcase. In her hand, she often has a coffee cake, or some sweet thing to share with her office. Thus burdened, she somehow manages to get the front door open, turns around to give me a kiss and saying, 'I'm off to save the world!' is gone.

"'I'm off to save the world.' She says it with a smile, and her tone is light-hearted. But Julia means it, too. She is happy. It's her life's work."

Julia and Will had been married for 33 years. During that time, Julia Vadala Taft became one of the country's top humanitarian relief experts, a friend and ally of the world's most impoverished people. Starting in 1975, when she directed the Indochina refugee task force, Julia essentially invented the way the United States government responds to natural and man-made disasters around the world, demanding basic rights for those whose lives are turned upside down by civil war, famine, religious persecution, earthquakes, floods and insect infestations.

Julia, whose career spanned the administrations of six presidents, died of colon cancer on March 15, 2008. She left a legacy of strategic vision and decisive leadership that will be celebrated for generations to come. "Julia was an image of American openness and generosity," said former Secretary of State Colin L. Powell, a friend and colleague for more than three decades. "Her professional life was committed to people trying to get by on a dollar a day, those who are hungry, without clean water, without medicine, without homes."[1]

Said retired General Wesley K. Clark, former supreme commander of NATO, and a friend and colleague for three decades: "Julia was a make-it-happen kind of a person. She knew how to get things done."[2]

A creative, compassionate woman, who married into a well-known Republican family—she wed William H. Taft IV, a great-grandson of President William H. Taft and a prominent member of the Nixon, Ford, Reagan, Bush I and Bush II administrations— Julia dedicated herself to restoring dignity and honor to those far less fortunate than she.

Julia's life was a portrait of inspiration and idealism in a world torn apart by ethnic hatred, terrorism, religious extremism, genocide and natural disaster. She knew how to tailor her mission to the troubles around her, when to call on the skills of the military to solve a problem and when to tap nongovernment experts. In a city filled with oversized egos bent on turf building, Julia was a builder of coalitions, determined to go for the right solution, not the easy one.

"She used her wit, passion, determination, knowledge and contacts to promote a humanitarian agenda—and succeeded," said Refugees International President Ken Bacon. "Julia was fearless about the bureaucracy. She knew how to make the power of the United States government work for her, and she didn't do it in a ruthless way that made enemies. People liked being ordered around by Julia Taft."[3]

Julia would tap her fat Rolodex of top officials whom she knew personally and professionally—Powell, Clark, Gerald Ford and George H.W. Bush, George Shultz, Caspar Weinberger, Elliot Richardson, Donald Rumsfeld, Richard Cheney, James Woolsey, Strobe Talbott, Richard Holbrooke, on and on—and tell them what strings to pull to get whatever she needed for the current mission: visas, military planes, armored convoys, search-and-rescue dogs, relief supplies, maps, intelligence briefings, tents.

Julia used her passion, energy and pragmatism and a revolving team of experts to find creative answers to complex humanitarian aid questions. And once she came up with a plan of action, she would use equal doses of chutzpah and charm to rally American and foreign VIPs to the cause. "Julia called herself an 'operations person' who was interested in the mechanics of protecting refugees and delivering life-saving aid," said Bacon, who died of cancer 17 months after Julia. "It was her ability to bring order to chaos—plus her willingness to get on a plane, helicopter, jeep or riverboat to go almost anywhere—that enabled her to make a difference. Whether in the White House or a governmental meeting or a refugee camp, Julia knew how to get people moving."[4]

Like many women in high-octane marriages, Julia juggled her responsibilities with those of her husband, Will Taft, who held one important administration appointment after another: principal assistant to Caspar "Cap" Weinberger, who was director of the Office of Management and Budget under President Nixon; general counsel to the Department of Health, Education and Welfare, under President Ford; deputy secretary of defense, under President Reagan; acting secretary of defense after George H.W. Bush became president; the United States permanent representative to NATO during the Gulf War; and legal adviser to Secretary of State Colin L. Powell under George W. Bush. Most of the positions Taft held were presidential appointments that required the consent of the Senate.

Julia and Will spent much of their married life in Washington, where they raised three children: Maria, born in 1976, William in 1978 and the youngest, Julia, named for her mother and known to all as Julie, born in 1980. One of the rules of the Taft household: no complaints. Maria once arrived home from boarding school and went into Julie's bathroom to take a shower. "There's no hot water," she yelled to her sister.

"I know," Julie replied. "There hasn't been any for months." When Maria asked why Julie hadn't told her parents, the teenager shrugged. "I didn't want to complain," she said.

Julia and Will made sure that each of their children did humanitarian work abroad, though the experiences didn't always turn out as planned. Maria was infected with malaria in Belize while building a bus shelter for a village with no road. William went to Kyrgyzstan to set up a computer center in a village with no electricity. Julie traveled with her mother to the Fourth World Conference on Women in Beijing. "Mom was on crutches with a sprained ankle, rain was pouring down, our clothes were covered with mud… and we couldn't have been happier," Julie said. Two years later, at 17, Julie asked her mother if she could spend the summer living and working in a refugee camp in Africa. "To some mothers, it may have been their worst nightmare," Julie said. "But to my Mom, it was a dream come true."

There was no one like Julia Taft. No one.

A tall, handsome, charismatic woman with perfect posture, deeply set dark eyes and thick, curly black hair that turned gradually to silver, Julia was a size 16—and proud of it. She had a regal presence with a personality that filled whatever room she was in. Her laugh, which started with her shoulders, was contagious. Her glare could make a general quake. When visiting a strict Muslim country where women are forbidden to make eye contact with men, she would look Taliban officials straight in the eye. And she loved being mistaken for Maude, played by Bea Arthur, in the long-running television sitcom of the same name.

Julia could converse in the acronym-littered *patois* of an inveterate Washington policy wonk, but she was quick to pick up the latest *National Enquirer* at her local supermarket. She had a weakness for caramel-filled chocolates, ordered popcorn with double butter at the movies and kept a box of Nabisco double-stuffed marshmallow cookies in her desk drawer. Although she was a spiritual woman, raised Episcopalian, Julia did not attend church regularly. Yet throughout her life, she believed in the power of prayer.

While she could be formal and formidable in public, she was witty and wacky with friends. After dinner at the family farm in Northern Virginia, she delighted in banging out "Blue Moon" on the piano. And at the end of a long evening, just as guests were ready to leave, she and Will would call everyone into the library for a round of Blockhead, a game that requires balancing colorful wooden shapes on top of each other to make a sculpture. It is, in effect, a genteel test of sobriety and would be played until everyone was ready for the drive home.

But when disaster struck somewhere in the world—whether in Vietnam, Armenia, Sarajevo or Kosovo, Afghanistan, Iraq, Ethiopia, Liberia or Sudan, Julia would drop everything to focus on her new, most vital effort. Better than anyone else, she knew how to make the often-intractable gears of bureaucracy shift into action, frequently before the president of the United States—whoever that was at the time—had decided to act.

Julia also knew how to speak truth to power. In December 1988, after she briefed President-elect George H.W. Bush on the American response to the Armenian earthquake, which she had directed, Bush told her he planned to send his son, Jeb, and grandson, George P. Bush, to the Soviet republic on Christmas Eve to hand out gifts to earthquake victims. Julia told Bush pointedly that Armenian officials had their hands full and had neither time nor resources to devote to foreign VIPs.

"And, by the way," she said, "the Armenians do not celebrate Christmas on December 25 but January 6." Bush sent his family on December 24 anyway.

"Julia was never a prisoner of ideology," said Ken Bacon. "She was an idealist who was always willing to make practical compromises. She would tolerate fools—and try to turn them around."[5] She was not always successful, but she was never deterred.

As was common in the 1970s and '80s, most of the top officials Julia dealt with were men who dominated the American and international foreign policy establishment and were often patronizing and dismissive of female colleagues. "Being a woman in these situations was unique," said Renee Bafalis, who served as Julia's press secretary for many years and often traveled overseas with her. "A lot of these world leaders were not used to dealing with a powerful woman. But Julia had the ability to take the most hardened leader and soften him up to the point where he was kissing her on the cheek when she left."[6]

Yet however powerful she may have appeared in meetings, at the end of a long day, Julia liked to relax at home with a bubble bath. When whatever she was reading fell into the water, she knew it was time to go to bed.

I met Julia Taft for the first time in 1971. She was a White House Fellow, a prestigious, one-year position for ambitious young men and women who want experience working at the highest levels of the federal government, and I was a young reporter with The Associated Press. I interviewed Julia, the only woman in the group, and wrote an AP story about the Fellows briefing President Nixon on their two-week trip to Latin America.

Julia and I met again professionally in Moscow in 1988, shortly after the Armenian earthquake. By then, she was a high-ranking State Department official, directing the American relief effort in the Soviet republic, and I was a foreign correspondent for *TIME* covering the story from Moscow. I attended a news conference Julia held in the Soviet capital before she returned to Washington. It would be almost 20 years before we would meet again, this time through our children.

My son, Christof Putzel, began dating the Tafts' younger daughter, Julie Taft, a charming, outgoing fellow Maret School graduate who, like Christof, shared a love for Africa. Julie had worked on a refugee project in Sierra Leone. Christof made his first documentary, called "Left Behind," about AIDS orphans in Kenya. As mothers, Julia and I enjoyed watching our children's romance flourish, and in the process, found we had many interests and friends in common.

Julia and Will's son, William, was already engaged. He had fallen in love with Begüm Bengü, a beautiful and talented Turkish-born architecture student, whom he had met at Yale when both were undergraduates. Begüm held a master's degree from Harvard. William was a law clerk for U.S. Court of Appeals Judge Samuel A. Alito Jr., then a nominee to the Supreme Court.

In August 2005, Julia and Will traveled to Istanbul at the invitation of William's future in-laws, Hasan and Beyhan Bengü. William had proposed to Begüm the previous February, and preparations were underway for a wedding to be held in Washington, D.C., in November. The purpose of this trip was to celebrate the engagement with Begüm's extended family and for Will and Julia to get to know Begüm's parents.

Julia was fully aware that Turkish culture had well-established rituals for formalizing engagements, and that as mother of the groom, she had an important role to play. It soon became clear that she was more familiar with many of these traditions than Begüm's parents, and perhaps more enthusiastic about acting them out than any of her future in-laws. She had obviously been looking forward to this for a long time.

It was not Julia's first time in Turkey. In the 1980s, she traveled with Will on a Defense Department trip to Troy and Ephesus. When describing the highlights of the journey, she recalled the shock of seeing an American tourist visiting Ephesus climb onto the amphitheater stage and begin to sing, "I'm a little lamby, yes I am'y." Julia would later pay homage to this gross breach of decorum by reenacting it at various amphitheaters in Greece and Sicily during later family trips.

Preparations for the pre-wedding trip to Istanbul began in Washington. Julia's research indicated that as the groom's parents, she and Will would be expected to give gifts of silver and chocolate to the parents of the bride. Flowers would be part of the package, but they could be procured in Istanbul. By chance, Begüm's anticipated monogram—B.B.T.

for Begüm Bengü Taft—matched that of Julia's mother-in-law: Barbara Bradfield Taft. A silver dish with Barbara's monogram was transported from Washington to Istanbul, together with a box of chocolates bearing pictures of the national monuments.

Once in Istanbul, Julia supplemented the Washington-themed chocolates with some fine selections purchased from the chocolatier in the lobby of the Swissôtel. (She always had great taste in chocolate, developed over the years through study and consumption of the Whitman's Sampler she always received as a Christmas present and honed during her years in Belgium.) Next came the flowers, an enormous arrangement exceeded in its beauty only by the logistical challenge it presented in transporting it from the hotel in Ortaköy across the Bosporus to the house of Begüm's parents, perched on the hillside above Anadoluhisarı.

Fortunately, help was on hand. Julia's godson, Jack Brown, was conducting research in Istanbul that month. He was given the task of transporting the flowers—by Istanbul taxicab—to the dinner party hosted by Hasan and Beyhan during the first night of the trip.

That night, during dinner under the stars at the Bengüs' home, Julia asked about the itinerary for the next day. There would be a cruise up the Bosporus, but before that, Julia wanted to make sure there would be a trip to the Grand Bazaar on Sultanahmet, near the famous Blue Mosque and Aya Sofia. She had to purchase a few more things to help "seal the deal" between the families.

The next evening, both families climbed aboard the *Lüfer II* ("The Bluefish II") for a cruise up the Bosporus. The weather was perfect. The boat crossed under the Sultan Mehmet II Bridge and made its way up to a small bay, a few turns below the entrance to the Black Sea, and anchored for dinner. At that point, Julia produced a small pouch of henna that she had purchased at the bazaar. Henna is traditionally applied to the hand of the betrothed woman to mark her engagement. The package did not come with instructions for preparing the ointment, but Beyhan's sister, Handan, with the help of one of the stewardesses on board, was quickly able to turn the powder into a clay-red indelible paste.

Following tradition, the mother-in-law is expected to bribe the bride-to-be to accept her son's proposal. No chocolates here—this was strictly a cash deal. Begüm held out her hand, fist closed, as Julia presented increasing, but nominal, amounts of money to induce her to accept. (Sometimes, cash is insufficient, and pieces of jewelry are needed to close the deal. Here that proved unnecessary. Although no receipt was kept, it is believed that William was "had" for 10 Turkish lira, about six U.S. dollars at the current exchange rate.) Finally, Begüm opened her hand, and Julia applied a spot of henna to her palm. Her mission to Istanbul was complete.

Will and Julia returned home relieved and happy that the trip had gone well and filled with excitement and anticipation about the upcoming nuptials. But the stars were not all aligned. That September, Julia learned she was battling a progressive form of colon cancer. She was 62 years old and had never had a colonoscopy. "I will fight this like the Taliban," she e-mailed me shortly after receiving the news.

And fight she did, beginning with the timing of her first chemo session, which she scheduled the week after William and Begüm's wedding on Saturday, November 5. On November 7, a hospital secretary called Julia to say her chemo treatments would start the following day, instead of Wednesday, as Julia had planned.

"How long do they last?" Julia asked.

"Six hours," the secretary replied.

"Six hours?" Julia said. "That's not convenient. I have a board meeting that morning with the Dalai Lama."

The secretary was unmoved. "That is the *doctor's* schedule," she replied. "He only does these chemo sessions on Tuesdays."

Julia was insistent. "I am also attending a lunch with the Dalai Lama and hosting a dinner for him," she said. "I can skip the lunch, but that's it."

The secretary reported Julia's unhappiness to the doctor and called her back: The doctor would start the treatments on Wednesday.

After learning that they would last for weeks, Julia decided that she would spend her "down" time writing a book about the highlights of her career. I offered to help and, over the next year, conducted a dozen taped interviews with her, each about an hour long. Julia concentrated on the intensity and excitement of directing some of the most complex humanitarian relief missions of the last three decades: her role as head of the task force that managed the resettlement of refugees from Vietnam, Laos and Cambodia in 1975 at the end of the Vietnam War; Operation Lifeline Sudan in 1988; her direction of the American relief effort during the Armenian earthquake, also in 1988; the Siege of Sarajevo, which started in April 1992 and lasted until February 1996; the crisis in Kosovo in 1998-99; and her trip to Afghanistan in 2001, when she worked for the United Nations.

Julia also talked about her fascinating and enduring friendship with the Dalai Lama, whom she met in 1999 when she was the State Department's coordinator for Tibetan issues and made an unprecedented trip to Dharamsala, high in the hills of northern India, where the Tibetan spiritual leader had established a government in exile.

She shared tapes of televised interviews she had done with ABC's Ted Koppel, PBS's Jim Lehrer, NBC's Jane Pauley and other well-known television personalities. She also provided the names of many government officials with whom she worked and traveled over the years. To my delight, when surfing the Internet one day, I found a lengthy oral history Julia had recorded in 1996 for the Library of Congress (LOC) as part of its American Memory Historical Collection. She had never mentioned it.

Woven together, the interviews, oral history and dozens of newspaper stories about her over the years offer a mosaic of a determined, hard-charging and idealistic woman who not only ran some of the most dramatic relief efforts of her generation but also influenced the debate at home and abroad as the international spotlight moved from Vietnam, Cambodia and Laos to the collapse of the Soviet Union to ethnic conflicts in the former Yugoslavia. Julia's story reflects the history of three decades of unrest and social upheaval in the 20th century, at home and abroad.

Throughout countless rounds of chemotherapy, Julia kept a full schedule, traveled extensively, spent a year commuting between one coast and the other, agreed to an interim appointment as chief executive of a large humanitarian organization and planned Julie and Christof's wedding. She coordinated every detail of the event, as if planning a state dinner. When I chose a lipstick red dress for the occasion, she insisted that I return it. The mother of the groom would follow the old adage to wear gray and keep her mouth shut!

On Saturday, June 2, 2007, at the Tafts' 14-acre farm in Lorton, Virginia, Julia took her son's arm and walked down what the family calls "The Staircase to Nowhere," a cascade of long cement steps that lead from the house to a field below, where 200 guests were putting to

Taft Farm.

Julia, on the arm of her son, Willim H. Taft V, decends the "Staircase to Nowhere" for the wedding of Julie & Christof on June 2, 2007.

Julia and Will Taft stand at the wedding.

Henry Putzel III officiates at the wedding of Julie & Christof.

Julia laughing at Will's bridal toast.

Wedding photos by Greg Gibson

good use the delicate pink hand fans Julia had had placed on each chair. The temperature had soared into the high 90s, and the sun was searing. But when Julia appeared—elegant in ice blue silk and smiling broadly— everyone broke into cheers, tears and applause. It's not every wedding that the mother of the bride gets a standing ovation!

Or that she shares in an elegant toast from the father of the bride. Julia beamed and her eyes glistened when Will Taft held high his champagne glass and addressed the two Julias in his life. "When we named Julie after her mother, we did so in the hope that she would be endowed with some of her mother's fine qualities, amongst them: loyalty, sincerity, a winning smile and an abiding concern for people who are less fortunate."

During our all-too-brief four years of friendship, Julia and I shared many confidences—about our lives, careers, families and, eventually, after the wedding, our dream of sharing grandchildren! It was a subject we never brought up with Julie and Christof, but we loved to discuss the possibility when we were alone. On our regular outings—for lunch, movies or just a manicure—we often stopped to gaze into baby store windows and debated which frilly dress or sailor suit we would buy first. In her heart, Julia may have realized that the odds were against her, but she never said so aloud, and she refused to give up hope. Even in her final months, Julia dreamed of one last adventure, maybe a safari in Africa with Will and the kids or another mission for the Dalai Lama.

That was the essence of Julia Taft. She was an eternal optimist. She had run countless disaster relief programs, and she would run this one.

Julia took enormous satisfaction in having her children launched— Maria with a master's in business administration from Stanford, concentrating on complex deals; William as an attorney with a fine law firm in New York, specializing in litigation; and Julie, with degrees in international relations and nursing, who was following in her mother's footsteps and would soon be working with refugees in some of the darkest corners of the globe. If only she could have lived to see her first grandchild, Ella Noor Taft, born to Begüm and William on December 4, 2008. Their second child, William Dennis Salim Taft, was born on September 18, 2011.

As Julia's cancer spread and her doctors tried new experimental drugs to slow it down, she railed against the expense of the treatments— some pills cost $88 each and were so big that she had to crush them with her garlic press—but she took them, if not always without complaint.

In June 2007, in the midst of yet another chemo session, Julia sat down at her dining room table and penned an op-ed piece for *The Washington Post*, criticizing the George W. Bush administration for its slow, reluctant resettlement of Iraqi refugees, many of whom faced death threats in their country because they had worked for U.S. forces. "What has happened to our leadership on this issue?" she wrote. "No matter your view of the war, welcoming the persecuted and standing by our friends is the right thing to do."[7]

In mid-summer, I accompanied Julia to Georgetown University Hospital for an appointment with Dr. John L. Marshall, the clinical director of oncology overseeing her chemo treatments. Dr. Marshall told Julia that he would be on vacation for two weeks in August and would see her again on August 28.

"I'm sorry, but I am moving to California on August 25," Julia said.

The doctor looked up from his papers, startled: "Say that again, please."

"I am moving to California on August 25. I was planning to go on August 20, but I can wait a few more days."

"Moving, like moving and taking your bed?" the doctor asked.

"Yes, moving," Julia replied. "Will has an appointment in California. Will is my husband." Will Taft had been offered a visiting professorship at Stanford Law School, and Julia had insisted that he accept it.

Undoubtedly, Dr. Marshall had a lot of cancer patients who wanted to pack up and leave at some point, but I doubt that anyone ever actually did so in the middle of such a critical treatment. But he didn't blink. "And where in California might this appointment be?" he asked with a hint of a smile.

"Stanford," Julia said matter-of-factly. "We will be in Palo Alto."

Dr. Marshall told Julia that he would arrange for her to see one of his colleagues at the University of California San Francisco (UCSF) School of Medicine. "I'll set it up," he said. And he did.

That fall, I visited Julia in Palo Alto and met her at UCSF, where she was having another treatment. The move had been difficult, but she was in good spirits. "Hey, Sweetie, do me a favor," she said as I arrived. "Run across the street to that little deli on the corner. I want the double pastrami sandwich on white, and the biggest piece of cake with icing that they have." She polished them all off!

Julia holding a machine gun in El Salvador, 1986. Photo courtesy of Taft family.

This was the beginning of a wonderful family Thanksgiving with Julie and Christof at their new apartment in San Francisco. Julia, as usual, organized everyone. At one point we went on an excursion to a tourist trap called the Mystery Spot in the woodsy hills near Santa Cruz, where buildings with tilted floors and slanted ceilings create the sense that the body is defying gravity. Julia had visited the place as a young girl

Julia with Colin Powell and Bernie Loeffke in China, 1983.

Julia and Will Taft in 1993.

Julia and Will Taft in 1984 at his swearing in as Deputy Secretary of Defense, accompanied by their children, Maria, William and Julie, and Will Taft's parents, Barbara and Bill Taft.

Photos courtesy of Taft family.

The Girls. Left to right: Maria Taft, Ann Blackman, Leila Fitzpatrick, Julia Taft, Julie Taft March 2007. Photo by Michael Putzel.

Margie Axtell, Ann Turner and Sue Woolsey with Julia in Hawaii, November 2007. Photo courtesy of Margaret Axtell.

Collage from Julia's 65th birthday. Left to right: Ellen Brown, Margaret Axtell, Ann Blackman, Sue Woolsey, Pat Goldman, Ellie Merrill, Leslie Ariail, Bobbie Kilberg. Photo Courtesy of Margaret Axtell.

Sheppie Abromowitz and Julia in broad brimmed hats. July 2007. Photo courtesy of Margaret Axtell.

and laughed uproariously as we all stumbled through it.

Julia still wanted to write her own book. She outlined a memoir that would combine the high points of her professional life with her pride in being a wife and mother. She had two titles: "A Decoupage of Disaster Response," and "A Kaleidoscope of Crisis Response." She purchased a red leather-bound volume with lined, blank pages and had begun to write in her careful, schoolgirl cursive: "While I neither aspire nor expect to be singled out as a super-mom/super-woman, the path my life has charted has been unusual, no, extraordinary.

"I have been blessed with strong family ties, close friendships and professional experiences spanning a spectrum of academic, governmental, non-profit and international arenas. As I currently face the drama of fighting cancer, it has become a personal goal that I capture the highlights of my life to pass on to my husband and children and to my friends who have been such an important part of my life."

That's all there was. Julia wouldn't admit it, but even if she had had more time and more energy, I doubt that she would ever have had the patience to sit in one place long enough to produce a book. (When I told her so, she stuck out her tongue at me.) Everyone who knew and loved her understood that she would never have been content writing about the circus. She wanted to be the ringmaster. She didn't want to pontificate about refugee problems. She wanted to go to the camps and reassure the people there that help was on the way.

So this will be, in its way, *our* book, and I will take my cues from Julia, as I always did. It is not intended to be a full biography or a grand history of the programs Julia administered. My objective has been much smaller in scope: to write down the stories Julia delighted in telling family and friends around the dinner table and put them into a short, historical context. Any material in quote marks comes from my interviews with Julia, her Library of Congress oral history, my many interviews with those who knew her and news articles about her work. The newly digitized archives of the *New York Times* and *Washington Post* have been treasure troves.

There are obvious drawbacks in writing about a friend, especially a member of one's extended family. It's impossible to be totally impartial, and impossible not to give a damn what friends and family think. And the politics can be tricky. But there are pluses as well, the key one

Julia in March 2007. Photo by Michael Putzel.

being access to loved ones, friends and colleagues who are eager to talk about someone they cherished and admired so deeply. They have given generously of their time, and I accept responsibility for any errors in the text.

Julia was no milquetoast, and she probably had her share of critics. I didn't dig too deeply. A number of her friends encouraged me to write a complete biography, warts and all, insisting that Julia deserved the best. I couldn't agree more. But there are times when it's important to put impartiality aside and concentrate on the essence of a life well lived.

So for this story, picture Julia sitting on the deck of the family's house in Washington, or stretched out on the chaise longue in her office nibbling chocolate, or perched on the screened porch at Indian Springs Farm, iced tea in hand, explaining how the U.S. government became involved in each humanitarian crisis, how she handled the inevitable bureaucratic snafus that developed, how she persuaded skeptical officials in foreign governments to cooperate and how she survived in some of the life-threatening situations she faced.

There are funny scenes, as well as poignant ones. Most of my interviews with Julia were interrupted two or three times by the ringing of her cell phone, which was never nearby. "Oh, where is that damned thing?" she would say each time. Then she would return to the tape recorder and pick up in mid-sentence, exactly where she left off. "This will be my legacy," Julia said in our last official interview. "Well, my kids are my legacy, but I need to leave this for my friends in the field."

CHAPTER 1

BEGINNINGS

Julia Ann Vadala was born on July 27, 1942, on Governors Island in New York Harbor, where her father, Colonel Anthony Joseph Vadala, was a surgeon in the Army Medical Corps.

Anthony Vadala, who was from Sicily and known to the family as Tony, immigrated to the United States in 1904 at the age of 12. He and his mother moved to Philadelphia, where he graduated from the University of Pennsylvania Medical School in 1916. Two years later, he joined the U.S. Army. Tony was raised as a Catholic, but when his first marriage ended in divorce, the church excommunicated him.

In 1937, Dr. Vadala, now an Army colonel, met Shirley Harris, a small-town girl from Loveland, Colorado, a sleepy town 50 miles north of Denver known as America's "Sweetheart City." Shirley, who had been raised Episcopalian, had been a music student, an aspiring violinist and pianist. Her father was a farmer who later worked for the State Farm insurance company.

When Colorado Women's College offered Shirley a scholarship of $35 a semester, she accepted it. Her parents borrowed a Ford from friends and drove their daughter to Denver with, as Shirley wrote later to her daughter, Julia, "one suitcase of clothes and a trunkful of dreams." She was determined to succeed in her new environment.[8]

Shirley was in her junior year when she met the sophisticated, wealthy Tony Vadala. He was 45. She was half his age, and he was dating her roommate, Miriam, a beauty queen. "He was her ticket, and later mine, to elegant dinner parties and a world of sophistication beyond the

Julia in her college years.

Julia Taft's college yearbook picture. 1964.

Photos courtesy of Taft family.

college compound," Shirley wrote. "When his attentions turned to me, rather than Miriam, I responded favorably out of a natural attractiveness to this worldly man, but also out of my hidden delight that he dumped the beauty queen for me."

Upon graduation, Shirley became a schoolteacher in Denver. Tony was eager to marry and have children. When he was transferred to San Francisco, he begged Shirley to join him. "He bought me elegant clothes to enhance my own maturing beauty and to insure his 'trophy' escort was appreciated by his circle of friends," Shirley wrote. "For a small town girl from Loveland, the future with Anthony seemed glamorous and secure."

When they were wed in a civil ceremony in San Francisco in 1939, Shirley sent her parents a terse telegram. "Tony and I were married today in S.F. I am content."

After the wedding, the couple moved to Panama, where Dr. Vadala was in charge of the ear, nose and throat department of Gorgas Hospital. At the time, Panama was a free port, and goods from all over the world were pouring in. The couple had fine furniture, a staff of seven and soon, a new son, whom they named Anthony.[9] "My mother wasn't exactly a hostess like Pearl Mesta," Julia told me, "but my father introduced her to some women who gave her an incredible education in the finer points of high society—how to choose linens and porcelains and antiques, and how to learn to dress, things she would never have learned in Colorado."[10]

A year later, they moved to Governors Island in New York, where Dr. Vadala became commanding officer of the army hospital at Fort Totten. Julia was born two years later.

The family soon moved to Denver, where Dr. Vadala was named head of the ear, nose and throat department at Fitzsimmons Army Hospital, which was used during World War II to treat returning casualties and became one of the country's premier medical training centers.

In 1950, when Julia was 8, her father was transferred to the 97th General Hospital in Frankfurt, and the family moved to Germany, where they lived until 1954. "They were magical years, because we were able to travel all over postwar Europe," Julia said. "We didn't have much money, but you didn't need a lot of money, and we had incredible experiences. My father, who spoke English, French, Italian and Spanish, taught us to try to understand other cultures."

During a visit to Rome when she was about 10, Julia was overwhelmed at seeing Pope Pius XII offer morning Mass in St. Peter's Square at the Vatican. "He was so serene and so calming," Julia said. "This was seven years after the war, and I think people were searching for religion. He came out in these white papal robes and radiated purity, and everyone looked at him in such a devout way that I thought, 'Gosh, this is good stuff. I should do this.'" During the visit, Julia found a Catholic publication that showed an altar in somebody's home, and she thought, "This is exactly what I need. I can do this." So when the family returned to Germany, she built an altar in her bedroom where she practiced giving sermons and performing religious ceremonies.

The family moved back to the United States when Julia was 12, settling in El Paso, Texas. Julia built an altar in her room there as well. "I was very, very devout," she explained. "It gave me a sense of well-being. And it has stayed with me—not the Catholic part, because we are Episcopalians—but the sense of grace you can feel without trying to be somebody you are not or without trying to impress other people."

The years living in Germany also gave Julia a lifelong love of travel. "You get it in your bones when you're young," she said.[11]

Julia graduated from Austin High School in El Paso and returned to Colorado, where she attended the University of Colorado in Boulder. She worked as a dormitory counselor to qualify for free room and board, served as a dean's assistant in advising freshmen and was business manager of the Coloradan yearbook. She was also a member of the Pi Sigma Alpha national political science honor society.

She joined a sorority and took classes Mondays, Wednesdays and Fridays so she could ski Tuesdays and Thursdays at Winter Park. She worked Saturdays as a waitress to pay for lift tickets, which cost $2.50 a day. She spent summers not far from home, waiting on tables in Estes Park, Colorado, which serves as the entrance to the Rocky Mountain National Park. Julia also dated a football player at the University of Wyoming named Fred Malone, the cousin of one of her sorority sisters. They would eventually fall in love.

In the summer of her junior year, Julia's parents took the family on a trip to Hawaii, Japan and the Philippines, a pre-college graduation trip. They had been home only a few months when Julia's father fell sick and died. The cause was liver cancer. He was 72. "Even as a full colonel, my father didn't make that much money," Julia said, "and my mother was terrified that she would be destitute. But she had death benefits, thank God, because we had no money. We had spent it all on travel."

Julia graduated in 1964 with a bachelor's degree in political science. "I adored college, I had so much fun, "she said. "Nobody had as much fun as I did."

CHAPTER 2

THE CIA: A SPY IS NOT BORN

After graduating from the University of Colorado, Julia and several sorority sisters moved to New York City, where she was hired by Radio Free Europe to work as an editorial assistant in the fundraising department. Six weeks after she started, her boss died of a heart attack, and Julia was assigned to clean out his office. "I was going through his files and found all these letters from the Central Intelligence Agency," she said. "I had no idea that Radio Free Europe Fund was connected with the CIA. Then I thought, 'This is pretty interesting stuff.' So I went back to graduate school and started my application to the CIA."

To her delight, Julia passed the written test and was asked to visit the agency's headquarters in Langley, Virginia, for more testing and a personal interview. "I thought, Mata Hari, this is the life for me," Julia said. "I was so excited." She and other applicants were told to report on a given date to the Albert Pick Hotel in downtown Washington, where a bus would pick them up at 7 a.m. They were to talk to no one on the bus. "We had three days of interviews, and some of the tests were the stupidest I've ever gone through," Julia said. Some were multiple choice, such as:

"Do you ever get mad at your parents? Always. Sometimes. Never.

"Do you ever get air sick? Always. Sometimes. Never."

Julia didn't want to appear compulsive, so she checked "Sometimes" for every answer. When she was finished and turned in the test, a voice came on to the loudspeaker telling her to report to a psychiatrist in the main office. When she arrived, he said, "You really blew it. The test shows you qualify as a paranoid schizophrenic."

Julia was irate. "That was the stupidest test in the whole world," she said with characteristic bluntness. "I checked the middle box every time because I thought if I checked 'always' or 'never,' you'd think I was obsessive." After several minutes of conversation, the officer decided that despite the test results, Julia was actually "normal," whatever normal meant to the CIA. She also passed the required lie detector test. But during the process, Julia decided she was not cut out to be a spy.

In 1966, she returned to Colorado to marry her old boyfriend, Fred Malone. He had been writing to her while she was in New York and was now working at the International House of Pancakes to earn money to attend law school. But the marriage was doomed before the knot was tied. "He was funny and wonderful and charmed the pants off everyone," Julia said, "but I later found out he was a con artist, a sociopath who had no connection to reality and no sense of guilt."

Fred also had no sense about money. "He figured as long as he had blank checks, there must be money in the bank to cover them," Julia said.[12]

Two days before the wedding, scheduled for September 10, 1966, IHOP fired Malone. Julia already had been having misgivings about the marriage—Malone had disappointed her many times—and she was angry. When she arrived at the church in her frilly white wedding dress—with guests already seated in the pews—Julia decided not to go through with it: "All my friends said, 'You're just nervous.' I said, 'No, I don't want to marry this guy. He has disappointed me. I don't want to marry him.' I refused to go down the aisle. I wouldn't go."

Julia's mother was sitting outside the rector's office when the minister approached and asked that she tell her daughter she was making a mistake. "I'm not going to tell her that," Shirley Vadala replied. "If she doesn't want to marry him, she doesn't have to marry him." Then she looked the minister in the eye and said, "Don't make her marry him."

Julia's girlfriends, however, were horrified. They told her that they had purchased dresses for the occasion, and they had no doubt that Fred would make a fine husband. "He was not fine," Julia told me. "But 20 minutes later, I walked down the aisle on my brother's arm." Within 18 months, they divorced. "We had no children," Julia said, "and it was time to get out of Boulder."[13]

Julia had enrolled in graduate school and was working on a master's degree in Middle Eastern studies. She completed the course work and, at the last minute, started a thesis on the Arab nationalist movement and the tensions between the United Arab Republic and Israel. "I spent two weeks totally in seclusion writing this thing," she said. "No TV, nothing. My basic thesis was that Egypt and Israel needed each other to be able to galvanize support for their own existence. This tension was what kept them from having a war."

Julia delivered the thesis to her adviser at 5 p.m. on June 6, 1967. "I got in my car, turned on the radio and found that war had broken out between Israel and Egypt. It was the beginning of the Six-Day War, and my whole theory had fallen apart." At that point she decided she would never be a good political theorist![14]

One day Julia was reading an article in the *Chronicle of Higher Education* and saw an advertisement for the White House Fellows, a leadership program for talented young people who work as special assistants to top White House officials and Cabinet members. She sent away for an application, but when it arrived, she was bowled over by the required credentials. "I knew I couldn't measure up," she said. "They wanted to know not only what your degrees were in, but how many countries you'd consulted with, how many books you had written, what kinds of community activities you were leading in, and so I put it away and wrote on my calendar that the next year I should send away for the application again."[15]

And she set to work lining up those credentials.

First, she decided to finish her degree and chose the terror of Stalinism as her new thesis topic. "I figured that he was dead. I'm not going to get caught up in the Middle East crap anymore," she concluded. "I've never been able to figure out the Middle East since."[16]

Then Julia took a job in Denver with the Western Interstate Commission for Higher Education, a nonprofit agency devoted to promoting cooperation to improve educational programs and opportunities in western states. She was responsible for a program that developed continuing education programs for library personnel, including one for Hispanic communities. She worked also with a program assisting Idaho, Montana, Nevada and Wyoming to use community hospitals as clinical teaching sites and recruit doctors to work in sparsely populated areas of the West. This would be the spark that ignited her interest in humanitarian relief programs.[17]

Julia wrote several professional publications about how to organize primary health care services in rural areas of the United States. She discussed the kinds of extension services needed to deliver care, basing her work on ancient Chinese tradition: bring medical care to the local village and teach people to be self-reliant. "We had midwifery programs and others in which we tried to arrange for specialists in medical schools to come out and see what practical family medicine ought to look like," Julia said. "We were thinking about how to look at the health care profession to see what people really need. We found they need preventive health care; they need the family; and they need the patient to be the leader of the team, not the doctor always being the decision maker."[18]

She completed her thesis on Stalin and received a master's degree in political science. To check off the "community service" box, she coordinated a political science lecture series, worked with a program that provided educational experience for high school dropouts and helped the Boulder Civic Opera with its fundraising strategy.[19] Then she sent away again for a White House Fellows application.

CHAPTER 3

WHITE HOUSE FELLOWS

More than 4,000 men and women applied for the 1970-71 White House Fellows year. Seventeen would be chosen. The 12-page application, which would be used by the FBI to do a thorough background check of the finalists for a top-secret security clearance, required listing educational background, college activities and degrees; employers, jobs, supervisors, work description, salaries, and references. A written essay was required as well. Hudson B. Drake, who was director of the program that year, put together a team of government readers to screen the applicants. Four readers went over each application and narrowed down the pool to about 150, the names of whom were sent to 10 regional panels whose members were appointed by the president of the United States. The interview process was rigorous.

Julia Vadala was one of 31 national finalists—and one of only two women.

They were invited for three days of intensive interviews at Airlie House, a historic conference center in the Virginia countryside, about an hour's drive from Washington. It was the second weekend in May 1970.

Two weeks earlier, on April 30, President Nixon announced that American forces had invaded Cambodia. On May 4, Ohio National Guardsmen opened fire on an anti-war demonstration at Kent State University, killing four students. Across the country, dissent disintegrated into a nationwide student strike, and many college campuses closed.

That weekend, 100,000 anti-war protesters convened on Washington, chanting "Hell no, we won't go" as they marched defiantly down

Pennsylvania Avenue. Police ringed the White House fence with buses to block demonstrators from breaking into the Executive Mansion. Crowds of students plowed into the buses, trying to roll them over. "You could hear the rattling of the buses inside the White House," said Bobbie Greene Kilberg, who was a White House Fellow at the time and had an office in the basement of the West Wing.

Several of the 15 presidential commissioners on the selection committee to interview the finalists had to drop out at the last minute. Father Theodore Hesburgh, chairman of the Civil Rights Commission and president of the University of Notre Dame, stayed on campus: there had been rumors that the ROTC building would be firebombed. He delivered a speech condemning violent protest but called for withdrawal from Vietnam. (Nixon later fired Hesburgh from the Civil Rights Commission because he criticized the administration's civil rights record.)

Most finalists arrived at Airlie by chartered bus. When boarding, they were given a booklet listing each person's name and résumé. Everyone was on edge. "As we drove down the highway, I read that one finalist, George Heilmeier, had already invented the liquid crystal display," said Marshall C. Turner Jr., a biomedical engineer who, at 28, was no slouch himself. With a heart surgeon, he had developed an implantable left ventricular heart assist pump. Turner was one of two finalists from Harvard Business School. "After reading through the one-page biographies on the bus, I didn't think I had a prayer," he said. Most felt the same way.

Julia knew no one. And at 27, she was among the youngest in the group. The only other female finalist was Patricia Goldman, who had been working in Washington since graduating from college. Pat was the director of manpower and poverty programs at the Chamber of Commerce, as well as one of the leaders of the Ripon Society, a political organization for liberal Republicans. "I'll never forget the first time I saw Julia," said Pat, who roomed with her that weekend. "Here was this tall, beautiful woman, teetering down a gravel driveway in high heels, next to another finalist, an Air Force officer named Dick Klass, a decorated Vietnam vet, who was considerably shorter and struggling with her suitcase."

The White House Fellows program has a venerable history. Proposed originally by John W. Gardner in 1957, when he was president of the

Carnegie Corporation, the idea was to bring talented young leaders to Washington to work for a year at the highest levels of government. They would be paired with senior White House officials and Cabinet secretaries, who would act as mentors and help them learn the challenges and complexities of governing. Gardner's vision was that the Fellows would return to their communities with top-level experience and contacts and become the next generation of leaders.

It took seven years for the idea to take hold. In 1964, when Gardner was president of the Carnegie Corporation, he proposed the idea again, this time to President Lyndon B. Johnson. The new president embraced it enthusiastically. "LBJ invited the Fellows to the White House often," said Marshall Turner. "He would call at 2 a.m. and say, 'Come on over for bridge.'"

Distinguished White House Fellow alumni include Doris Kearns Goodwin, a Pulitzer Prize-winning biographer; Tom Johnson, former publisher of the *Los Angeles Times*; Timothy E. Wirth, former senator from Colorado; Henry Cisneros, former secretary of Housing and Urban Development; Bobbie Greene Kilberg, CEO of the Northern Virginia Technology Council, who served in the Nixon, Ford and Bush I administrations and married a Fellow from her class, Bill Kilberg, an employment and pension lawyer, who became a senior partner in the law firm Gibson, Dunn & Crutcher; Colin L. Powell, former secretary of state; and Wes Clark, former supreme commander of NATO.

One of the strengths of the program is that it often acts as a springboard, launching Fellows to a higher level of positions and opportunities than might have normally been available to them. "The program didn't change my career path, but it greatly accelerated it," said Hudson Drake, who was a manager in the aerospace industry when he came to Washington at the age of 29 to be a White House Fellow. After four years of top experience in the federal government, he skipped several management levels and returned to the private sector as vice president and general manager of a defense electronics company. "In military parlance, this would be akin to jumping from the enlisted ladder to the officer's ladder, moving from a Navy petty office to a senior commissioned officer," Drake said. "It just doesn't happen. But it did!"[20]

That would be true for Julia as well.

Throughout the three-day interview process at Airlie House, which former Fellow Frank Gannon described as "a weekend that only Evelyn Waugh and Agatha Christie could do justice to,"[21] finalists met individually and in pairs with commission members and their wives. Commissioners that year included Robert Abplanalp, who invented the aerosol valve, a conservative Republican who was a close friend of Nixon's; Kenneth Cole, Nixon's domestic policy adviser; Patrick J. Buchanan, a Nixon speechwriter; Doris Kearns; and Vera Glaser, a syndicated columnist with the North American Newspaper Alliance.

At each meal, finalists were seated next to a commissioner or a commissioner's spouse and grilled about all aspects of their lives. Pat Goldman said that at one point Abplanalp turned to her and said, "I'll bet you can't type."[22] Another commissioner, W. Glenn Campbell, a conservative economist who helped build the Hoover Institution at Stanford University into an influential conservative research group, found a dozen different ways to ask finalists if they had ever smoked dope.

On Sunday night, the commission voted. The finalists went to bed at Airlie House not knowing if they had been selected. The next morning, still with no news of the outcome, the group boarded a bus and returned to Washington. As they got off, each person was handed an envelope with an acceptance or rejection inside. "Everyone read the letter and then looked up to see stunned faces around them," said Turner, recalling the moment 40 years later. "Many of the men had wives meeting them at the bus. We didn't know what to say to each other. It was absolutely brutal."

Julia was selected. Marshall Turner was chosen as well. So were George H. Heilmeier, who, at 33, already held 10 patents; West Pointer Dana G. Mead, 32, one of the youngest lieutenant colonels in the Army, who had served as operations officer for the northernmost American unit in Vietnam that tried to block the North Vietnamese from crossing the demilitarized zone and infiltrating the South; J. Keith Crisco, 27, a Harvard Business School graduate who directed a small business consulting service for minority businesses in Greensboro, North Carolina; Richard L. Klass, 29, an Air Force captain and Rhodes scholar, who had served in combat in Vietnam during the Tet offensive and the battle of Khe Sanh; and Leon A. "Bud" Edney, 35, a Naval Academy graduate with the rank of lieutenant commander, a fighter pilot, who had made two deployments to Vietnam and flown 200 combat missions over

North Vietnam. They would join the fifth class of White House Fellows.

Pat Goldman was not accepted into the program. Whatever the reason, she was exceedingly gracious about the loss and asked Julia to move in with her while she looked for an apartment. They would become lifelong friends.

"There were 17 of us, and Julia was the only woman," said Turner. "But she was comfortable with being tall, and she was always very much at ease. She became our leader, the heart and soul of our group." Most of the men were married, and Julia, who enjoyed having girlfriends, sought out their wives. "She was open and irreverent and didn't wear her intelligence on her sleeve," said Turner's wife, Ann, an artist. "I had two children under five and sometimes was a little uneasy around accomplished women, but I never felt that way around Julia. She was easy to kick back with."

Ann Turner said that her husband once called Julia when he was out of town and asked her to go to their home and help Ann, who was receiving threatening phone calls from a stalker. "Julia answered one call and whatever she said to this guy, he never called back," Ann said. [23]

Acceptance letters in hand, the new class of Fellows and the commissioners walked directly from the bus to the White House to have their pictures taken in the Oval Office with President Nixon. When they arrived, they were told to line up in the lobby, behind a group of savings and loan executives who would also be shaking hands with the president.

Marshall Turner had been raised in La Habra Heights, California, near Yorba Linda, where the president grew up. When Turner's introduction came, he told Nixon that his family had shopped in the grocery store run by the president's parents. Nixon, who had appeared tired, suddenly became animated. "You know what my job was in the store?" he asked Turner. "Freshening the lettuce." Nixon explained that he would mix a small amount of high-quality motor oil in a can with water and then spray the lettuce. "Made it look nice and shiny," the president said.

Only H.R. "Bob" Haldeman, who was standing nearby, knew why Nixon may have seemed a bit off that morning. Hours before, the president had made a strange, pre-dawn visit to the Lincoln Memorial to talk with anti-war activists camped out on the steps. Bobbie Greene, a White House Fellow that year, accompanied him. A White House operator had called her at 2 a.m. to say that Nixon wanted her to report

President Nixon greets White House Fellows in Oval Office on Monday, May 11, 1970. That morning, right after the White House Fellows program completed its selection process for the class of 1970-'71, the new class was ushered over to the White House to meet Nixon. Photo Credit: White House Fellows brochure, 1970-'71. Courtesy of Marshall Turner.

Cabinet Room: Julia Taft was the only woman at the table when the White House Fellows briefed President Nixon on December 22, 1970, about their trip to South America. Photo Credit: White House Fellows brochure, 1970-'71. Courtesy of Marshall Turner. White House photo archived at the Richard Nixon Presidential Library and Museum.

to the White House immediately. "I rarely saw the president and couldn't imagine why I was being asked to come down to the White House in the middle of the night," said Bobbie. When she and several other young White House staffers arrived, a guard directed them to the South Portico, the back door of the White House, where John Ehrlichman, who was Nixon's chief domestic adviser and Bobbie's boss, ushered them into a car in the waiting motorcade for the short ride to the Mall.

"Nixon talked for an hour with a group of drowsy but astonished demonstrators," according to *TIME*'s account. "His discussion rambled over the sights of the world that he had seen—Mexico City, the Moscow ballet, the cities of India. When the conversation turned to the war, Nixon told the students: 'I know you think we are a bunch of so and so's.' Before he left, Nixon said: 'I know you want to get the war over. Sure you came here to demonstrate and shout your slogans on the ellipse. That's all right. Just keep it peaceful. Have a good time in Washington, and don't go away bitter.'"[24]

Years later, Bobbie recalled: "The president tried so hard to relate to them. In trying to find some common ground, he began to talk about football, but then he realized that these protesters were the least likely group to know about sports."

The day that started with a bus ride from Airlie House and a photo session with the president of the United States ended back at the White House theater, where the new class of Fellows and spouses were invited for cocktails and a movie.

The Fellows' wives were included in some functions, but most of the activities scheduled for them centered on coffees, teas and luncheons with the wives of Cabinet officers, senators and military officers. In a handbook written for the next year's session and illustrated by Ann Turner, program officials suggested that before coming to Washington, the wives use the summer "to get in some serious reading on the functioning of your government." They were told that in order to familiarize themselves with the names and issues in the news, they should subscribe to the *Washington Post*, the *Evening Star* and the *New York Times*. "The first two are good for locating housing possibilities," the manual added.

In a section on etiquette, the wives learned: "It's always a good idea to have a pair of white gloves with you for emergencies during day and evening. Hats are no longer worn." In another section, headlined "To

Work or Not to Work," the manual stated: "There is never any objection to a wife working during the year. Each wife must assess the program planned in terms of her own needs and then make her decision."[25]

In truth, whether women should work at all, especially if they were married with children, was a subject of hot debate. The women's liberation movement was propelling more and more women into the workplace and into positions with titles that had long been held by men. The divorce rate soared as couples who married with one set of expectations found their hopes and dreams diverging. Some *über*-feminists stopped wearing bras and shaving their legs. Men questioned whether it was still considered polite to hold open a door for a woman.

Having grown up an Army brat, Julia was always comfortable in the company of men. "This was very early in our awareness of gender issues," she said in an oral history of her life recorded by the Library of Congress in 1996. "But I had no trouble at all. I've always thought of my gender as an asset. I've never been apologetic. I've never been angry. I've always worked with men, and I enjoy working with men. The Fellows treated me like a little sister. They'd say, 'Go out of the room because we're telling dirty jokes.' But in fact, it was very rare to have a woman high up with access to Cabinet officers. We've come a long way since then."[26]

Depending on their background and experience, the Fellows were paid around $15,000, then a GS-9 on the government pay scale, which was intended to keep federal salaries commensurate with those at a similar level in the private sector. That year the GS-9 was about the same as annual salaries of first-year associates in New York law firms.

Julia's new income allowed her to rent an apartment on the first floor of a small brick house on 29th Street, just off Connecticut Avenue and not too far from downtown Washington. "We had a lot of parties there," Pat Goldman said. "Julia liked theme parties and loved to dance. One weekend we sent out invitations to a rock 'n' roll party."

The Fellows met several times each week for seminars, often over breakfast, lunch or dinner at the home of a Cabinet secretary, where they discussed the issues of the day and how they cut across different government agencies. *Washington Post* publisher Katharine Graham invited them for dinner. They made four trips to New York City to study the electoral process and social issues; met with FBI Director J. Edgar Hoover; visited the LBJ ranch; watched the launch of Apollo XIV, which made the third lunar landing, commanded by astronaut Alan Shepard Jr.; spent a day underwater in a nuclear submarine; and toured West Virginia for three days with Secretary of State Jay Rockefeller, who took them to see a strip mine. "It was a dream year, unbelievably rich," Turner said.

Julia was assigned to the office of Vice President Spiro T. Agnew, a former governor of Maryland, who two years later was charged with extortion, tax fraud and accepting bribes totaling more than $100,000 and forced to resign. "He was quite something," Julia said in her LOC oral history. "He was chairman of the National Council on Indian Opportunity, but he didn't care anything about Indians. Coming from the West, I thought they were terrific." Julia worked on a policy to turn management, ownership and responsibility of reservations over to the Native Americans.

At first, Julia was impressed with Agnew, a tall, bullet-headed man who was such a newcomer to the national stage that when Nixon selected him to be his vice president, pundits asked: "Spiro who?" "We later found out he was a crook," Julia said. "But he was a wonderful speaker. He wrote and gave speeches that were so polemical. He really crystallized issues. He was very colorful in his speech…and he really resonated with the conservatives."[27]

Nixon himself considered Agnew somewhat of a buffoon, with little understanding of his role or sensitivity about his relationship to the president, always pestering him for better staff and better perks of office. But as anger mounted over the growing toll of the Vietnam War, Nixon found that he could turn his vice president into an attack dog, unleashing him to slam liberal critics and the media as "the effete corps of impudent snobs" and "nattering nabobs of negativism," phrases crafted for Agnew by Nixon's bombastic speechwriters, Pat Buchanan and William Safire.

Agnew had been frustrated by the tedious study required in dealing with such substantive issues as health care and Native Americans and relished his new role in the spotlight. "All of this period was very difficult because of the war protesters," Julia said in her oral history, "and Agnew got on his high horse condemning them. He alienated himself from the academic community and from the youth of the country. It was really incredible. But as a person he was quite nice. He did spend an awful lot of time in Palm Springs vacationing with Frank Sinatra. I did not think

[Agnew] was an extremely serious man."[28]

Through her involvement with Indian issues, Julia met Kilberg. Bobbie was a staff assistant to the president, concentrating on domestic issues. Her responsibilities included Native Americans, and she and Julia often found themselves working together.

In October 1970, Julia and Bobbie attended a convention of Native Americans in Anchorage, Alaska. Afterwards they boarded the Teapot Dome train, once used by President Warren G. Harding and now restored to its original luster, for a 12-hour train ride to Fairbanks. Along the way, they dined on fresh Alaskan shrimp, lobster and crab, served on silver platters by uniformed waiters. Then they boarded a prop plane and flew 170 miles to the tiny village of Tanana, home of a native Alaskan named Morris "Maury" Thompson, who was a special assistant to Interior Secretary Walter J. Hickel, a former governor of Alaska. Thompson was working in the Department of the Interior and wanted them to see where he grew up. But Thompson had given the village elders the wrong arrival date, and when the White House party arrived at the narrow airstrip, no one was around to greet them. "There was snow on the ground, and we walked a mile into town," Bobbie said. "All along the way, we ran into people who shouted 'The Anglos are coming! The Anglos are coming!'" By the time they arrived at the community center, villagers had gathered, and Julia and Bobbie sat on the floor with elderly Native American women who wrapped them in colorful blankets to keep warm.

A few hours later, their pilot appeared and announced that a major storm was brewing and that they must leave immediately or be snowed in for several days. Someone suggested that because they were so near the Arctic Circle, they should fly there first so they could have bragging rights of having crossed it. "It was the bumpiest ride of my life," Bobbie said.

Exactly two years later, in October 1972, the same pilot was carrying Louisiana Rep. Hale Boggs, Alaska Rep. Nick Begich and a Begich aide on a flight from Anchorage to Juneau when the plane disappeared. Neither the wreckage nor the remains of the four people on board were ever found.

In December, the Fellows took a two-week trip to Latin America to meet with government officials, educators and businessmen, as well as cultural and labor leaders. They were divided into two groups, and each visited five countries. Julia went to Guatemala, Argentina, Mexico, Panama and Peru. "We saw governments which can't respond to the needs of the people," Julia said in an interview with me shortly after I had arrived in Washington as a young reporter for the Associated Press. "In Peru and Guatemala, the governments appear to be unwilling to integrate the Indians into their political structure. I came back more tolerant of the United States because I had the perspective of seeing frustrations Latin Americans face on a day-to-day basis. I was glad to come back to a government with a president who seemed to be reaching out to listen to us."[29]

And Nixon *did* listen to them! After the Fellows returned from their trip to the Southern Hemisphere, Julia suggested that they write a report on their findings for Nixon and maybe he would meet with them. "Classic Julia," said Marshall Turner. "She came up with a great way to get a substantive meeting with the president." The White House scheduled them for a late afternoon session in the Cabinet Room on December 22 with National Security Adviser Henry Kissinger and told them Nixon might "drop by." At the last minute, however, Kissinger canceled and Alexander Haig, who was Kissinger's deputy, became the substitute.

Moments later, they were startled when a doorman announced, "Ladies and gentlemen, the president of the United States," and in walked Nixon. Just as the Fellows completed their remarks about South America, Kissinger joined them unexpectedly, leaned over and whispered something into Nixon's ear. Several Fellows insisted afterwards that they heard the word "China." And they might have been right. Six days earlier, Kissinger had hand-delivered a message from Chinese Premier Chou En-Lai to the Pakistani ambassador about the possibility of Nixon's visiting Peking, so it is possible he had just received a reply. Whatever the case, for the rest of the meeting, the president was in an expansive mood.

He spent more than an hour discussing foreign affairs, ranging from country to country, mesmerizing his audience. "A surprise part was his occasional profanity," Marshall Turner said. "At one point, he contrasted the likely futures of the Philippines and Indonesia, one country with a strong American presence and one without, and talked about the Nixon Doctrine. Leaning back in his chair, he summed it all up by saying: 'What the Nixon Doctrine boils down to is that most countries are fucked up pretty much in direct proportion to the American presence there over the years.'" Deeply impressed at the sweep and detail of the president's commentary, the Fellows asked each other, "Why doesn't he speak that clearly on television?" (Without the profanity, of course!)

At another point in the discussion, Nixon asked the Fellows if they had been to the Soviet Union. "You haven't been to the USSR?" he said. "Henry, they have to go to Russia."

Kissinger made it happen. In June 1971, most of the group took off for the USSR, Romania and Yugoslavia, where they met with communist youth groups, collective farmers, labor leaders and Soviet government officials. At the last minute, the Soviets denied visas to the four Fellows in the military, two of whom spoke Russian. Instead, they traveled to NATO bases to investigate drug use and joined the Fellows on the other legs of the trip. [30]

Throughout that spring, there were anti-war marches and rallies in Washington almost every weekend. Julia attended one of the larger demonstrations. When she reported for work the following Monday, a member of the vice president's staff asked what she had done that weekend.

"I was just around," Julia said.

"Around where?" the man replied.

"Around D.C., I didn't go out of town. Why?" said Julia.

"I know where you were," the man snapped. "You were on the Mall. I saw your face on TV. I want you to know it is unacceptable for anyone on the vice president's staff to be seen at an event like that, and you will not do it again." [31]

Despite the turbulence of Nixon's first term, it was probably the White House Fellows program that first impressed Julia with the importance of networking, which was not yet a verb. During that first year in Washington, she met people she would know and work with throughout her life. They climbed the rungs of the career ladder together, often suggesting each other for government and non-government positions, sometimes butting heads with old friends, occasionally delivering disappointing professional news, attending the weddings of each other's children, and at the end of their professional runs, helping a younger generation with job contacts. "It was a wonderful learning experience and a wonderful personal one, because we all stayed in touch over the years," Julia said.

Just as John Gardner hoped, the fifth year of White House Fellows went on to become accomplished leaders in their own communities and professions. George Heilmeier continued a distinguished career in technology and engineering by becoming director of the Defense Advanced Research Projects Agency, chief technology officer of Texas Instruments and CEO of Bellcore (now Telcordia Technologies), and by now the owner of 15 patents; Dana Mead became CEO of Tenneco and chairman of the board of MIT; Keith Crisco was founder of an elastics company with offices in seven countries and later was named North Carolina's secretary of commerce; Dick Klass spent 22 years in the Air Force and retired with the rank of colonel; and Bud Edney became commandant of the Naval Academy, commander of the Atlantic Fleet and vice chief of naval operations, the No. 2 job in the Navy, retiring as a four-star admiral. Marshall Turner became an early-stage technology venture capitalist and CEO of several technology companies, including DuPont Photomasks Inc. He also served as chairman of the Corporation of Public Broadcasting and of the National Museum of Natural History. Earlier in his career, he was CEO of a start-up company that developed a temperature-sensitive liquid crystal display used in the mood ring!

"The Nixon administration had so much bad happen to it after our year," Turner said 40-plus years later, "and Nixon's place in history is so over-defined by Watergate—the voice on the tapes and associated opprobrium—that it's hard to place oneself back in the 1970-71 time period. It was a very substance-driven administration that we were excited to be part of. The attitude was to redo the Great Society as much as possible, but with better legislation and results. We all felt we had the opportunity to be taken seriously at the highest levels if we had a good idea, and many of us had that experience."[32]

When the fifth class of White House Fellows ended in the fall of 1971, Elliot Richardson, who was Nixon's secretary of health, education and welfare, offered Julia a position that would make use of her background in the delivery of health care to developing areas. She was interested but told Richardson that she needed to think about it. She was considering work overseas, perhaps with the Peace Corps. "I thought I was good at organizing and motivating people and really was interested in the social service question," she said in her oral history. "I wanted to meet people who were doing community-based programs and the kind of work I thought I could do."

Julia spent six weeks that fall traveling in Africa, mainly Nigeria, Kenya and Tanzania, where she met with U.N. workers, Peace Corps volunteers, UNESCO employees, CARE officials, missionaries—as many people as she could find delivering health care to rural populations. She also went on a hunting safari and can be seen in one photograph standing next to a dead zebra. At some point during the trip, she decided she wanted to work in a place where she could see something changing as a result of her own efforts. "I got excited about what's happening in Washington," she said. "I saw that one person really can make a difference."[33]

Julia returned to Washington and accepted the job with Elliot Richardson at HEW. She was 29 years old and on the way up.

Julia takes a camel ride during a trip to Egypt in 1971.
Photo courtesy of Taft family.

CHAPTER 4

LOVE, WATERGATE & HEW

Sue Woolsey was working in HEW's Office of Planning and Evaluation when she and her colleagues heard some scuttlebutt that someone who had been on Agnew's staff would be assigned to the department. "We thought we were hot stuff, young kids doing important government work," Sue said. "We wondered how someone who worked for Agnew could possibly be serious."

This was long before the vice president resigned in disgrace, but the former Maryland governor had by then become Nixon's political attack dog and was widely regarded as highly divisive.

The first time Sue saw Julia, she was walking into a senior staff meeting at the department. "Here was this vision in peach silk," Sue said. "We all decided that this must be Julia Vadala." It was.

Julia was hired at HEW in September 1971, serving as special assistant for external affairs to Secretary Elliot Richardson, a cultivated, principled Republican who would go on to hold four Cabinet posts, more than anyone else in history. Julia's job was to act as a liaison with other departments, labor unions, educational organizations, welfare groups, nongovernmental organizations (NGOs) and minority groups.

"That first position and her later appointment as deputy assistant secretary for human development gave her an entree to deal with the entire human services side of HEW," said Stephen Kurzman, who was assistant secretary for legislation, the department's chief lobbyist on Capitol Hill. "We had the biggest budget after the Department of Defense, and it included all the social service programs for children, welfare recipients, the elderly and the disabled. Julia's exposure to those programs provided the groundwork for her later appointment as HEW's point person for resettlement in the U.S. of thousands of Vietnamese and Cambodian refugees, who desperately needed services of all kinds." [34]

When she arrived at HEW, Julia shared an office temporarily with Frank Samuel, who was Kurzman's deputy. With welfare reform and a national health insurance bill at the forefront of Nixon's domestic agenda, their office, right around the corner from the secretary's suite, was a hub of activity. "The two biggest initiatives of the Nixon administration were in our department," Samuel said. "It was an exciting time." [35]

And a busy one. Although welfare reform and national health insurance were ultimately not adopted by Congress, Julia's job was to brief interest groups on the administration's proposals in these areas and in many others. "It was a very hard sell," Kurzman said. "Many of these groups and much of the Democratic-controlled Congress were hostile to anything proposed by the Nixon administration." Even so, they had some important legislative victories—a safety net for low-income elderly and disabled people with the Supplemental Security Income program, major new investment in cancer research, incentives for health maintenance organizations and Food and Drug Administration (FDA) regulation of medical devices.[36]

Unbeknownst to all but a small team of White House operatives, a secret political operation about to unfold in the capital would lead to one of the most painful chapters in American history. On June 17, 1972, five men were caught breaking into the national headquarters of the Democratic Party, the political opposition housed in the Watergate office complex. Soon after, two young *Washington Post* reporters, Bob Woodward and Carl Bernstein, linked the burglars to the White House. Less than a month before the presidential election, the *Post* reported that the FBI had established that the break-in was part of a political spying and sabotage effort conducted by Nixon's re-election campaign, the Committee for the Re-election of the President, later nicknamed CREEP.

The public paid little attention to the scandal, which Ron Ziegler, the president's press secretary, called a "third-rate burglary attempt." On November 7, Nixon was re-elected by one of the greatest margins in American history, defeating South Dakota Senator George McGovern, the peace candidate. With a landslide like that, Julia concluded, "We didn't have to worry about all this Watergate stuff."[37]

On the heels of his electoral mandate, Nixon decided to shuffle his Cabinet. He named Elliot Richardson secretary of defense and moved Caspar Weinberger, who had been director of the Office of Management and Budget, to HEW. Julia wanted to go to the Pentagon with Richardson, but he insisted that she stay at HEW to help the new secretary get established. "It's important for Weinberger to understand what the interest groups believe and what this process has been," Richardson told her.

Weinberger brought along his top aide from OMB, a youthful Yale graduate with a law degree from Harvard, as his new executive assistant. His name was William H. Taft IV, and his great-grandfather was a Republican legend, the only person to ever serve as both president and chief justice of the United States.

Will Taft had worked for two summers as one of "Nader's Raiders," a small group of mostly Ivy League lawyers hired by consumer maverick Ralph Nader. They had spent one of those summers working on a report critical of the Federal Trade Commission, and when Weinberger was appointed to head the FTC in 1970, he had asked Nader to recommend someone to serve on his staff. Taft went to work for Weinberger and would follow him from one top administration post to another.

Tall with long, curly blond hair, Taft had a quick wit and a love of literature and opera. He owned a small, narrow (12-foot wide!) row house on A Street, not far from the Capitol. He frequently entertained, and his friends considered him a good cook. While waiting for dinner, guests enjoyed reading the magazines Will used as placemats.

Julia said that when she and Will met in November 1972, she was intrigued. "I'd go into his office in the morning, and he would be reading poetry," she said. "I thought, 'this guy's really neat.'"

She decided to check him out. "During the next few months, I needed to explain what it was I did, and I worked closely with Mr. Taft," Julia said in her LOC oral history. Sitting in her backyard with me, she put it less formally: "I tried to charm him and told him how absolutely essential I was with all the interest groups, and Will took notes."

Julia and Will dated quietly for 15 months. "They were so discreet about their romance," said Steve Kurzman, who became a lifelong friend. "Cap Weinberger had an 8 a.m. meeting every day with senior staff that included Will Taft and me, and I probably saw Will and Julia six times a day. I had no idea they were dating."

Frank Samuel and his Dutch-born wife, Jacqueline, weren't in on the secret either. But the two couples often had dinner together and, as Jacqueline says, "We had our suspicions."

Julia's mother, Shirley Vadala, then close to 60 and the widow of an Army surgeon, was in declining health. She had developed mouth cancer and came to Washington for treatment at Walter Reed Army Hospital, where Julia visited her regularly. "Shirley was a real character," said Jacqueline Samuel. "She had a great sense of humor." One day a group of medical students was seated in the hospital's amphitheater, where Shirley Vadala was Exhibit A, sitting on a chair on stage. Her surgeon had outlined with dye the area of her face and neck where he planned an operation to remove part of her jaw. As he lowered his patient's gown for a technical explanation, the students gasped in astonishment. Across her chest, Shirley had scrawled in red lipstick: "Go Redskins." The students gave her a standing ovation.[38] Shirley died in her home in Loveland, Colorado, in February 1982. She was 65.

Julia had been wrong to conclude that the administration didn't have to worry about Watergate. Woodward and Bernstein, eventually joined by a media gaggle, kept up a steady drumbeat of exposés into 1973. The Senate Watergate Committee, led by Senator Sam Ervin of North Carolina, launched a summer-long public hearing, dramatically televised on network television, to investigate the scandal. Even before the hearings began, Nixon was compelled to accept the resignations of his most loyal and trusted aides, chief of staff H.R. Haldeman and presidential counselor John Ehrlichman, although they steadfastly denied any wrongdoing in the affair. Nixon fired his White House counsel, John W. Dean III, who later confessed to the Ervin committee that he had participated in the high-level conspiracy to cover up senior involvement in the break-in. His riveting recitation of closed-door meetings led to Nixon's resignation a year later. Haldeman and Ehrlichman were convicted of conspiracy and obstruction of justice and served 18 months in prison.

As depressing and distracting as the daily Watergate headlines were to members of the administration, dedicated aides in the departments were proud of their work. "Putting Watergate aside, it was one of the most active periods of domestic policy legislation that we have ever seen," said Frank Samuel.[39]

At some point, Julia moved from 29th Street to a $334-a-month, two-bedroom apartment in a white brick building overlooking the Calvert Street Bridge and Rock Creek Park below. *Money* magazine featured her in a four-page spread that included a detailed breakdown of her $26,000 annual income, including budget and savings.

"Miss Vadala lives well," wrote *Money* correspondent Patricia Tucker. "She arrives at work at 7:30 a.m. and doesn't get home until 7:30 p.m., usually just in time to put on an evening dress and act as HEW's representative at one or more of the inevitable formal dinners that members of Congress and the diplomatic corps attend."

Under the headline "Sitting Pretty," the magazine itemized Julia's spending: around $3,800 a year in rent, $1,300 on vacations, $833 on gifts, $814 on clothing, $771 on food, $553 for car expenses, $378 for a color TV, $202 on liquor, $159 on dry cleaning and $61 on hair. "She buys what she needs and most of whatever else she wants," Tucker wrote. "She stashes any left-over funds in a savings account." That year Julia's "leftovers" amounted to $3,569.

For vacation, Julia was considering either a tour of Antarctica or three weeks in Crete: "She is so busy that she is unable to indulge her passions for travel, skiing and tennis." Julia also told Tucker that her hobbies included tennis and bike riding, but when *Money*'s editors asked her to pose for pictures, Julia had to borrow a racket, a white tennis outfit and a bicycle from her friend Pat Goldman. (The magazine did not use those pictures.)

As part of the feature package, *Money* provided Julia with three financial specialists, including Julia Walsh, who was a respected vice president of a brokerage company and a director of Washington's First National Bank. Walsh and the others advised Julia how to invest and, now that she had a respectable income, how to get her finances under control. "Her outlays for clothes were low for a woman in such a visible position; they will probably go up in 1973," Tucker wrote. "Her natural wavy hair kept her hairdressers' bills down. Vacations were high, she acknowledged—and were going to stay that way. Travel meant a lot to her, and she had no intention of cutting down unless forced to. The same goes for personal gifts."

Julia, who liked to ski, asked if buying a condominium apartment in a ski area would be a good investment. The advisers said that buying a house to live in would make more sense than buying a vacation place in a ski resort. "I don't know that I want to buy a house," Julia replied. "I have a friend who bought a house, and she doesn't have time for any fun at all now."

Julia did need to buy a new car. Her 6-year-old Chevy Camaro had died the day before the *Money* interview, probably because she had driven it for 18,000 miles without changing the oil. "The mechanic got so mad at me," Julia told the magazine. "He said, 'Lady, you wouldn't think of wearing a girdle for 18,000 miles without changing it, would you?'" Julia said that in Colorado, she would leave the car at the filling station and tell them to do whatever it needed. But when she did that in Washington, her bill was $190. "Since then, I've been ignoring maintenance," she said.[40]

Julia moved again in 1973, this time from Calvert Street into a small coach house in the Cleveland Park section of Washington, a historic, leafy community within easy reach of downtown. And on Valentine's Day 1974, Will Taft asked her to marry him. Three months later —May 4, 1974—they had a small wedding in the Georgetown garden of Taft family friends, followed by a larger luncheon and formal reception with dancing at the fashionable F Street Club in Foggy Bottom, near the State Department. "It was a very sunny day, and I remember Steve Kurzman dancing up a storm," Jacqueline Samuel recalled years later.[41] The bride wore a ruffled, peach-colored dress. "It was a short courtship, but it was very nice," Julia told me. "The reason it worked so well is that at first I saw him in a totally unromantic way."

Julia and Will Taft were married for the rest of her life.

CHAPTER 5

INDOCHINESE REFUGEE RESETTLEMENT

In August 1974, President Nixon resigned in the wake of the Watergate scandal and Gerald R. Ford became president. Less than a month later, Ford issued an unconditional pardon to Nixon for any offenses he may have committed. The decision proved a political disaster for Ford and unleashed waves of scrutiny and controversy that plagued his presidency and would be debated for years to come.

By March and early April of 1975, U.S. policy in Vietnam was in chaos. Ambassador Graham Martin was still pleading for more money to stave off the onslaught from the North Vietnamese, but many in-country foreign service officers, as well as officials on Kissinger's staff, were sending back-channel messages that South Vietnam was about to unravel and that the United States should begin an evacuation.

"The American public was very divided over the war," said Julia, who was deputy assistant secretary for human development at HEW with a portfolio that included Head Start, the aging, the handicapped, mental retardation and vulnerable children. "We had a Republican president and a Democratic Congress, very high unemployment, a sense of defeat, our first major defeat, politically and militarily because in South Vietnam, the Communists took over. There was a lot of rancor."

One day a friend who had adopted two Vietnamese children called Julia to say that she knew people in the process of adopting Vietnamese orphans and asked if the U.S. government had any plans to help them if Vietnam fell. "What does this have to do with me?" Julia asked.

"You can do something," her friend said, reminding Julia that her portfolio included vulnerable children.

Julia placed a call to a colleague at the State Department's Agency for International Development (USAID), the development arm that administers foreign civilian aid, and asked if anyone was paying attention to Vietnamese orphans. The query resulted in an action plan named Operation Babylift.

On April 3, with Saigon on the verge of collapse, President Ford announced that the United States would fly some of the estimated 70,000 orphans out of Vietnam with $2 million from a special foreign aid children's fund. The U.S. planned 30 flights to evacuate babies and children.[42] The first flight left Saigon's Tan Son Nhut Airport with 328 people aboard shortly after 4 p.m. on April 4. Twelve minutes into the flight, there was an explosion on board, and while the pilot managed to bring the plane down in a rice paddy, it broke apart. Only 175 survived. "I woke up to the news that one of the planes had crashed," Julia said. "We were just seared."[43]

Over the next few weeks, Operation Babylift brought 3,300 children out of Vietnam, all to be adopted by American, Canadian, European and Australian families. Julia said that the crash prompted a whole new evaluation of emergency evacuations, especially when children would be involved. "We had to learn about how to deal with pediatric requirements because up to then, almost everything was about how to care for adults," she said.

On Saturday afternoon, April 19, 1975, Julia was working in her downtown office—not unusual for a young, ambitious staffer—when a memo arrived from the State Department stating that there would be a 4 p.m. meeting of all Cabinet heads to discuss the evacuation of Vietnam. Weinberger was not in the office, and a USAID administrator asked Julia to take his place. She went home, changed into business attire, left Will a note saying that she'd be back later and drove to the State Department. It was the first time she had been involved in a meeting of this importance, and she was thrilled.

President Ford had established a task force of about 100 people from the various agencies—State, Defense, Labor, the CIA, the Immigration and Naturalization Service (INS), and HEW—to direct the evacuation and appointed L. Dean Brown, a former undersecretary for management at State, to run it. Henry Kissinger, who as Ford's secretary of state wielded enormous power, had called the last-minute meeting, and Julia worked all weekend to help put the task force in place.

The following Monday, she walked into Weinberger's office to ask if she could serve as HEW's representative to the team. Weinberger agreed.

When Saigon finally fell on April 30, 1975, hundreds of thousands of South Vietnamese who had sided with the United States were in jeopardy. Chaos and panic ensued as whole families tried to flee by planes, helicopters and boats that met merchant or military ships at sea. At the State Department's operations center, the interagency task force went into overdrive, working in around-the-clock shifts.

On May 27, President Ford named Julia to be director of the task force. With no background in foreign policy and no experience with Vietnam, she was not an obvious choice for the assignment. Yet at 32, with an impressive salary of $36,000—known at the time as a GS-17 or Super Grade—she became one of the youngest women to hold a top federal position.

This was the start of Julia's humanitarian aid career, but she had little time to savor the promotion and settle into her new job. The first planeload of 341 Vietnamese refugees was scheduled to arrive in the United States for resettlement the next day.

Julia's first official duty was to welcome the refugees at Fort Indiantown Gap, a sprawling military base surrounded by forests and hills in Pennsylvania Dutch farm country. With a contingent of Washington officials and politicians, she waited on the tarmac for the American Airlines jumbo jet to land. "They waited and waited," Larry Clinton Thompson wrote in a history of the evacuation. "Undaunted, Governor Milton Sharp proceeded to give a speech of welcoming to the new arrivals—who hadn't yet arrived."[44]

Julia found herself standing next to General Leonard F. "Chappy" Chapman Jr., Jr., who had been commandant of the United States Marine Corps during its bloodiest battles in Vietnam and then supervised the Marines' withdrawal from the country in 1971. Now head of the Immigration and Naturalization Service, Chapman was skeptical about the prospects for settling Vietnamese in the United States and made no secret of his position. "These people are going to be wearing loincloths and carrying spears," he told Julia. "I don't think we want any of them here. They're fighters."

Julia was nervous. She knew the refugees' evacuation from Saigon had been traumatic, that most had left the country with only what they were wearing and that they had lived for weeks in a dusty tent city in Guam. Would Americans see a line of dirty, ragtag Vietnamese exit the plane and not want to welcome them into their homes and communities?

What neither Julia nor Chapman knew was that before the refugees had boarded the plane in Guam for their long trip to the United States, someone in the U.S. military had understood the importance of first impressions and ordered everyone to be fitted with a new outfit—suits for men and the traditional flowing *ao dais* for women. When the plane door opened and the first Vietnamese family stepped out, the crowd responded with delight. "I'm telling you, these refugees could have been on the cover of *People* magazine," Julia told me. "These were people with whom Americans could identify."[45] Chapman was impressed as well. "They are wonderful people, and they are going to be good Americans," he told Julia the next day. "I didn't see anyone who looked like they'd be wild or murderers or anything like that."[46]

The next month, *People* featured Julia in a story titled "Women Power." "I really threw myself into it," Julia said of her new position. The article included a photo of the new task force director smiling broadly and holding a Vietnamese child in her arms.[47]

The resettlement of Indochina refugees may be one of the few success stories in the United States' sorry history of the Vietnam War. Over a period of seven months, Julia directed the relocation of more than 131,000 Vietnamese and Cambodian refugees in camps around the country, as well as on Guam and Wake Island and in Thailand. Congress appropriated more than $300 million for voluntary organizations, religious groups and local communities to feed and assist the refugees, as well as to find them jobs.

"The same kind of political debates that were going on in government plagued our churches and synagogues," Julia told me. "But when the refugees came, everyone put that behind them and said, 'We have to help these people start over again.' It was a very healing process. People had real tasks to do. Where are these people going to live? Did anyone have a car to loan them? What kind of school could they attend? Who could help them with health care?"

Not everyone was enthusiastic. Many Americans were under

the impression that the refugees were prostitutes, drug dealers and criminals. And rumors circulated that the refugees carried strange, contagious, Asian diseases from which Americans had no immunity. "This fueled a lot of opposition from some communities about accepting the refugees into their midst," said Robert V. Keeley, deputy director of the task force. "We did our best to contradict this rumor, but not always successfully."[48] California Governor Jerry Brown was fiercely opposed to having refugees come to Camp Pendleton. "We don't want these people," he told Julia. "We have enough people in California, and we don't need any Vietnamese."

Julia had a different view. "We had to show that the refugees were worthy of coming and worthy of us saving them," she said in her oral history. "It was important that we could document that nobody was on a blacklist, anybody's blacklist."

To coordinate security clearances and to make sure all refugee lists were identical, Julia appointed one person to work with seven agencies, including the FBI, the Drug Enforcement Administration, the INS, the CIA and the Defense Intelligence Agency. "This was a bureaucratic nightmare," Julia said. "The INS had most of its information on 3-by-5 cards, and the CIA had lost most of its records in Vietnam. So it was rather spotty, but we did make a major effort to find out what we could. With the assistance of an IBM computer program, which the company gave us free of charge—the Department of Social Security told us it would take them five years to do this—we figured out how to track all these people, many with the same or similar names. We had family identifiers, age identifiers, and name identifiers. Once we got the system in place, we were able to show that there were very few who had security hits, and we dealt with those separately. Then we started processing people out."[49]

Less than two weeks after Julia's appointment, Massachusetts Senator Edward M. Kennedy, who was holding hearings on the plight of the refugees, charged that the program had turned into a "shambles" because of a "failure of leadership." The report, submitted to the Judiciary Subcommittee on Refugees and Escapees, accused the task force of creating "bureaucratic roadblocks" and, according to the *New York Times*, "delaying resettlement of the bulk of refugees evacuated in April and May from Cambodia and South Vietnam." When *Times* reporter David Binder asked Julia for comment, she fired back at Kennedy with a litany of resettlement numbers: Of the 131,210 refugees in the system, 30,340 had been processed and released for settlement in the United States; 3,405 had been sent to other countries to live; there were 56,557 refugees in four American relocation centers; 43,158 at camps on Guam and Wake Island and in Thailand and the Philippines; and 1,045 were on their way to the continental United States. "That's pretty impressive, we think," Julia said.[50] Julia's numbers added up to more than the 131,210 refugees she said were in the system.

Binder, a friend of the Tafts, did Julia a favor with the story. The reporter could have produced a simple "he said-she said" piece. But instead, he pointed out that Kennedy had not done Julia the courtesy of showing her the 52-page report before releasing it to the press. Nor did the report mention that the INS had imposed strict security checks on the refugees, which was a major cause in processing delays. Binder wrote also that the House had "warmly praised the work of the task force."[51] In her first major assignment, Julia learned a key lesson about operating in the nation's capital—the importance of establishing a good relationship with the news media.

Julia also established a close relationship with one of the refugee families. "Bà (Aunt) Taft helped us in so many ways," said Minh Le, whose parents, Binh Van Le and Ninh Le Pham, arrived at Indiantown Gap with their eight children, all between the ages of 2 and 13, on the first planeload of refugees. The family had lived in DaNang, where Le had worked as a political analyst for the American General Consulate in Vietnam for 20 years.

With their government falling, Ninh flew to Saigon with the children. Not knowing if her husband would make it out of the country alive and fearing that she could not raise them alone in a foreign country, she went to the U.S. Embassy in Saigon to give up all eight of her children for adoption in America. But when she received news that her husband had just fled DaNang on the last boat, Ninh and her children flew to Guam. Binh and his family were later reunited at Camp Pendleton. When they arrived in the U.S., Binh went to the State Department to look for a job and was hired by Julia's resettlement task force.

"Bà Taft helped introduce us to American culture," Minh Le said years later. "Both Ong (Uncle) and Bà Taft became my parents' support system at a time when we were all struggling to start a new life in the

U.S." Julia and Will Taft admired the way the Le parents disciplined their children and hired Ninh to help care for their three kids. "Bà Taft helped my parents rent a house, which wasn't easy for a refugee family with eight children," Minh said. "She ordered catered Vietnamese food from my mother, who was known in the Vietnamese community for her specialty dishes. Bà Taft took us to the zoo, showed us how to ride horses at their farm and taught us how to decorate a Christmas tree with chains of popcorn and construction paper rings."

The Tafts made an effort to attend every celebration in the Le family. They were guests at the wedding of Huong Le, the eldest of the Le's, who had helped care for Maria Taft when she was a child. In 1993, when Minh's brother, Quan V. Le, became the first of three dentists in the Le family to graduate from the Virginia Commonwealth University (VCU) School of Dentistry, Julia, Will and Julie celebrated with the family in Virginia. It was just before Minh left home to start her first year at the University of Miami School of Law. She graduated in 1996.[52]

Inevitably, the resettlement program had problems. Some 1,600 Vietnamese refugees who had been evacuated to Guam, mostly military personnel who had worked with Americans, insisted that they did not want to leave their families in Vietnam and be resettled in the United States. They demonstrated, rioted and even tried to burn down their barracks, asking to be given an abandoned Vietnamese ship in the Guam harbor to transport themselves home. Julia prepared to fly to Guam to deal with the crisis, but when White House officials learned of her plan, they nixed it and ordered that someone with a lower profile undertake the controversial mission.

Julia turned to Bob Keeley, her deputy, and told him to fly to Guam in her place. But there was a problem. They had no time to buy Keeley a new plane ticket. "With a great big smile, she handed me her ticket and told me to figure out how I would explain to the airlines why I was using a ticket made out to Julia Taft," Keeley said.

"At least you will be flying first class, which as deputy director you would not rate," Julia told Keeley, who made it to Guam and back without being detained. Keeley also credits Julia's persuasive powers for the fact that these Vietnamese "repatriates," as they called themselves, did get their ship and returned to Vietnam. "After Henry Kissinger declined to authorize the usual repatriation, Julia took it up with President Ford and obtained his OK," Keeley said.[53]

Julia also quietly invested some of the remaining task force funds in an ongoing program to interview and resettle Indochinese refugees stranded in Thailand and other Southeast Asian countries. This "Expanded Parole Program" took in some 11,000 Indochinese refugees to the United States in 1976 and set a key precedent for a continuing program to resettle Indochinese refugees in America. "There were many battles in the years ahead, and Julia's longtime friend and associate, Shep Lowman, directed the Indochinese refugee program in Washington with extraordinary commitment and capability," said Lionel Rosenblatt, who headed the task force's office of special concerns and later became president of Refugees International. "The Carter administration responded generously to the growing refugee crisis—with the late Richard Holbrooke playing a key role. Ultimately, about 1.5 million refugees from Vietnam, Laos and Cambodia were resettled around the world—with about 1 million coming to the U.S. and greatly enhancing our country."[54]

Years later, Julia said that the key to her success was the unconditional support of President Ford. "If DOD or any agency was giving us a problem, I would go to Dick Cheney, who was Ford's deputy chief of staff, or Don Rumsfeld, who was chief of staff, and say, 'You've got to get these people off my back. We've got to make this thing work.'"

And they did.

CHAPTER 6

AQUARIUS

In January 1976, Julia and seven other women began meeting monthly for dinner and—most importantly—to share their experiences of motherhood. Some of their husbands had formed a book group the previous August that they named Leo for the astrological sign of their first meeting. The women decided to form their own group. "Most of us were introduced by our husbands," said Sue Woolsey, whose husband, Jim Woolsey, was a friend of Will Taft's. "The fact that they were putting together a book group without us gave us plenty to talk about."

The women followed the astrological theme and named their group Aquarius, and over more than 30 years, they forged strong bonds that revolved around family and friendship. When an Aquarian had a problem—with children, health or her marriage—she often called another member of Aquarius.

Besides Julia and Sue Woolsey, the original group consisted of Margie Axtell, Jacqueline Samuel, Ellen Brown, Jane Holt and Louise Tucker, who was Jane's sister. Within a couple of years, Bobbie Greene Kilberg and Margot Humphrey joined as well. "Most of us had toddlers or were ready to pop," said Jacqueline Samuel, a psychologist, whose husband, Frank, had been a colleague of Julia and Will Taft at HEW. "We were all working, and our mothers were all far away. We attempted for a while to read and discuss books, but that resolve deteriorated, and we just talked about whatever was imminent in the child-bearing and child-rearing department."[55]

Sue Woolsey, who worked with Julia and Will at HEW, said that although they were all professional women with good educations, they had not learned enough about mothering to make it on their own. "We grew our own extended family," Sue said. "Over the years, we have shared many wonderful times—our joys and our frustrations, our illnesses and our losses."

A constant theme that ran through their lives was how to balance childcare with a career. "Julia took a few years off when she first had children," said Margie Axtell, an architect married to Russ Stevenson. "But when she worked, she always gave it her all. When she was at InterAction, [the U.S.-based alliance for international relief and development agencies], she complained about younger women who took maternity leave and didn't always put in the hours that she was willing to put in when they came back."[56]

Margot Humphrey, a telecommunications lawyer, remembered that at an Aquarius dinner years ago, Julia asked whether anyone had suggestions on dealing with sibling rivalry. "Unusually for the Aquarians, there weren't many suggestions," Margot said, "though some of us were also experiencing the problem in various ways. But my mother-in-law had sent me a set of children's books dealing with all sorts of common problems, including this one. I said I had no idea how helpful it would be, since Kate is an only child, but I gave her the book on that topic to try."

At the next meeting, an uncharacteristically frazzled Julia greeted Margot saying, "I'm returning your sibling rivalry book and thank you. But I have to tell you, *it didn't work!*"

As she recounted the incident, Margot said, "No, Aquarian efforts to help didn't always work. Yet I, for one, always found it enormously helpful just to know that other high-achieving women were swimming in the same soup."[57]

Another theme was how to deal with male colleagues and bosses who had no experience or interest in working with women. "We all thought of ourselves as pioneers proving we could do anything at least as well as the men, Julia especially," said Sue Woolsey. "I remember when she was appointed head of the Vietnamese Refugee Resettlement Project that she quickly had to establish her authority over a number of military and hard-bitten, old-line foreign aid officials, probably all men. She talked about how crucial it was that she had the absolute backing of the

Leo book club members with their wives on a trip to France. From left: Will Taft, Margie Axtell, Jacqueline Samuel, Russ Stevenson, John Hoff, Frank Samuel, Laura Hoff. Fall 2007.

Aquarius: Standing, left to right: Ellen Brown, Margot Humphrey, Bobbie Kilberg, Margie Axtell, Ann Blackman. Bottom row: Jacqueline Samuel, Louise Tucker, Julia Taft, Sue Woolsey. January 5, 2008.

Photos courtesy of Margaret Axtell

secretary of HEW (Cap Weinberger) and President Ford."

As in most groups, some of the women became closer friends than others. But most agree that Julia was the moving force behind Aquarius. "As with so many things, Julia kept us together," Sue Woolsey said.[58]

There were Thanksgiving parties at the Woolseys', Christmas celebrations at the Samuels' house, Easter egg hunts at the Taft farm and Fourth of July celebrations at the Axtell-Stevenson cottage in Annapolis. Some of the families took vacation trips to Florida and Caribbean cruises, as well as an annual fall trip to the historic Homestead in Virginia— where the nearly empty hotel assigned the families a whole wing for their children to range through—while theoretically learning about the fine arts of afternoon tea and ballroom dancing. "After the kids were in bed, the grown-ups always played charades," Margie said.[59]

Louise Tucker remembers the time Julia arrived at a December Aquarius dinner having recently returned from a trip to Jerusalem. She brought a small octagonal box covered in gold paper for each member of the group. "Each contained a gift of gold, frankincense and myrrh," Louise said. "It was a labor of love for her to have carried the boxes back on the plane for us. It honored both the occasion and our mutual friendship."[60]

For several summers, the Tafts and Browns joined the Samuels at a rented house in Bethany Beach, Delaware. Julia took charge of games for the children. There were candy necklaces for the girls and glow sticks for the boys. One summer she arranged for them to be in the town parade, and Ellen Brown made costumes. Lucinda Brown won first prize for being the most patriotic baby and was awarded the Lady Victory trophy, which she still has!

The Woolseys once threw a Halloween costume party with a "guns 'n' butter" theme to celebrate Will Taft's new job as deputy secretary of defense. Russ Stevenson, who had met Will Taft in law school, dressed in black and carried a plastic gun. Russ's wife, Margie Axtell, wore a four-foot-high cardboard creation that she painted to look like a pound box of Land O'Lakes butter. Julia later borrowed the costume and wore it to a board meeting where she knew she would see the Land O'Lakes company president, whom she probably hoped to persuade to concentrate on a humanitarian issue of concern to her at the time. "Pure Julia," Margie said.

The couples also helped take care of each other's children when one or another family was living abroad. During the 1980s, Ellen and Jonathan Brown were stationed in Dakar, Senegal, with the World Bank. When Ellen became pregnant with Katharine, her middle child, Ellen returned to Washington and stayed at the Tafts' farm in Northern Virginia, where they helped take care of her and drove her to the hospital when it was time to deliver. The Browns asked Julia to be godmother to their son, Jack, and Will to be Katharine's godfather.

"My brother and I spoke a pidgin combination of French, called Wolof, a native language of Senegal and English," wrote Katharine, who was a captain in the U.S. Army in Iraq when Julia died. "I guess Julia was too hard to pronounce for us language-confused kids, so we came up with a nickname for her. Since she was the tallest woman we had ever seen (our own mother being 5'2") and because she was like a mother to us, we called her Mommy Giraffe. Still to this day, even though we are in our 30s, we call her Mommy Giraffe whenever we remember her, and we still call her husband Daddy Will."

During a joint Taft /Woolsey family trip to Paris and Brussels over Christmas and New Year's in 1989-90, when Will Taft was ambassador to NATO, the group met in Paris. Julia had advanced the trip and provided everyone with an itinerary of events spaced in 20-minute intervals and printed on a laminated 3-by-5 card. She gave the group exactly 20 minutes at Versailles. Jim Woolsey, later to head the CIA, sabotaged the schedule by renting an audio phone and strolling through the palace and grounds at a slow pace. "Julia nearly killed him," Sue said. Julia also shortchanged an excursion to the Louvre to see the Mona Lisa and Venus de Milo so they would have time to tour the Paris sewer system, a visit arranged by Julia's brother, Tony.

Julia had previewed a number of nightclubs and reserved tables at a cabaret called La Belle Epoque, the only Parisian strip show she decided was tame enough for the children. "The entertainers, of course, got Will up on stage," Sue said. They put a blindfold on the American ambassador to NATO and sat him in a chair while topless dancers paraded around him. "Julia wanted to hide under the table," Sue said.

Julie, who was 9-years-old, was horrified. "This was definitely one of the more scarring events from my childhood," she said. "By the end of the number, my dad was sitting on stage with a glass of Champagne in one hand, a barely clad woman on his lap and a G-string on his head.

I was appalled several years later when I found the G-string, with the name 'La Belle Epoque' stitched across it packed in a box at the farm."[61]

The group headed to Brussels for New Year's, where they met with Will's brother, John Taft, and his fiancee, Chris, and they all partied at Truman Hall, an elegant Flemish country estate that is home to the NATO ambassador. "Maria was angry because her parents were about to ship her off to boarding school," Sue wrote in an e-mail, and Roquefort, a mangy sheep dog named because he smelled like the cheese, "was throwing up half-digested bunny rabbits on the black Chinese carpet in the foyer."[62] It was one of many trips they laughed more about afterwards than at the time.

In 1990, the Tafts, Browns and Samuels made a six-week trip to Italy. There were six adults and eight children, and a highlight was a visit to Mascali, Sicily, the ancestral village of Julia's father, Anthony Vadala. The Italian ambassador to NATO, a colleague of Will's in Brussels, arranged the Mascali visit and made it clear to local villagers that they should go all out for the occasion. And they did.

Julia, Will and their children arrived by helicopter, landing on the village football field. A school band, led by Julia and the mayor, escorted them in a parade across the town square to the town hall, where Julia delivered a speech in Italian. The weather was so hot—the temperature rose to over 100 degrees Fahrenheit—that the interpreter's makeup started to melt. Afterwards, everyone gathered at the local Catholic church, where the priest honored them by opening the reliquary that supposedly held the remains of St. Leonard of Noblac, the town's patron saint. Later, the Americans joined the mayor at his opulent villa on the slopes of Mount Etna for a large lunch. "It was extremely hot," said Julie, "and we didn't understand anything because it was all in Italian. Both Dad and Mom had interpreters, but the kids didn't."

Throughout their trip, the Tafts, Browns and Samuels tried to stay together in a three-car caravan, but they kept losing each other because the Browns would stop at every roadside store to buy Tuscan pottery and plates. "I remember we lost them outside of Todi for several hours," Julie said. "This was before cell phones."[63]

During the course of the trip, dinners fell into a well-established pattern. If one of the rooms booked at their hotel had a balcony or terrace, the group would assemble there for cocktails, prepared from stores of whiskey and gin that they transported in the cars. "This was preferable to having cocktails in the hotel bar because it reduced the risk of drink orders being lost in translation," said William, "such as when the kids ordered Oranginas and were served a round of gin and orange juice."

After cocktails, the group would head to the hotel dining room. Regardless of the day of the week, the hotel restaurant would always be hosting a wedding party, especially in Sicily and Southern Italy, and the bride and groom would send over packets of candied almonds to the kids. One night, entirely unprompted, Julia took in the scene and told the table, "not all brides are happy."

No one ever knew what she was talking about, and even she confessed she could not entirely explain her commentary. "This happened a few nights in a row," William said. "After the second or third dinner wedding, before the candied almonds had even been sent over, the table would begin speculating about whether that night's bride was, or was not, happy." It would be many years before Julia's children learned that she had been unhappy at her first wedding.[64]

Julia may have had her share of setbacks, but she had an uncanny ability to focus her energy on all that lay ahead. Sue Woolsey put it best in her eulogy: "Julia wove ties of extraordinary strength with many of those she encountered in her life. She treated us to her warmth, her exuberance, good humor, compassion, and fierce determination to act for good. At least as much as her wide sweep on the world stage, these ties are her legacy."[65]

Julia was not the first Aquarian to be mourned. Of the nine longtime members, two others died prematurely as well: Jane Holt, of cancer in 2007; Ellen Brown, of a stroke on her way home to D.C. from Chad in June 2010. In a few short years, the small group had lost a third of its club. The Aquarians continue to hold their dinners, but they will never be the same.[66]

CHAPTER 7

OPERATION LIFELINE SUDAN

In September 1988, a colleague showed Julia horrific photographs of millions of people starving and homeless in southern Sudan. An estimated 250,000 Sudanese had died the year before because food deliveries were held up by both the government and Southern rebels, who had been fighting for six years. An estimated 3 million to 5 million people were starving, and several million more were refugees who fled their country to find food and avoid the civil strife.

Julia was now director of the United States Office of Foreign Disaster Assistance (OFDA), appointed by President Ronald Reagan. She headed a staff of 21 full-time workers who, as part of the Agency for International Development, were in charge of identifying the need for help and coordinating the federal government's response. Their operations center was located in a first-floor corner of the State Department. "It was there, usually around a gray, horseshoe-shaped battery of desks and telephones, that daily life and death decisions are made to deploy the planes that carry all matter of relief to victims almost anywhere in the world," Robert D. Hershey Jr., wrote in the *New York Times*.[67]

Julia had been working part time since the children had been born, and juggling her new, full-time position would not be easy. When she became director of OFDA in 1986, Maria was almost 10; William, 8, and Julie, 6. Her husband, Will, had recently been named deputy secretary of defense, a position that carried enormous responsibility and made it necessary to work long hours. "If by any chance on the same day we had an earthquake in country X, and there was a nuclear submarine off somewhere where it was not supposed to be, Will and I would have to be in our various offices," Julia said. "So we would either take the kids to work or drop them off with the Browns or the Samuels. I think it was kind of hard on them, but there was also an awful lot of excitement. I'd bring them to the office on Saturdays and snow days, and I think they got a sense of the immediacy. It was pretty heady stuff."[68]

When Julia learned that millions were starving in Sudan, she called Chester A. Crocker, assistant secretary of state for African affairs. "Chet, we need to do something about this," Julia said.

"The main problem behind this suffering is the continuing conflict between the North and the South," Crocker replied. "That is what we are trying to address."

"I need to focus on the humanitarian side," Julia said, "and it's my understanding that the government is not only preventing assistance from getting to the South, but they are not even willing to give assistance to the North." She was frustrated that the State Department was not pushing harder on the government of Sudan to feed its people.

"Up to that time, relief organizations did not openly provide assistance within conflict areas unless asked to by the host government," said William Garvelink, who worked on the Sudan situation at OFDA with Julia. "It was not acceptable to violate a nation's sovereignty."

With news reports showing the crisis worsening, Julia took the tape of a powerful NBC report on the situation to State Department spokesman Chuck Redman, who had been her next-door neighbor, and insisted that Redman deliver it to Secretary of State George Shultz before he met with the Sudanese foreign minister the following day. "I want him to know that the foreign minister's government is starving these people," she told Redman.

That afternoon, Shultz called Julia and Chet Crocker to his office. "So it was Chuck and me and Shultz and Chet who watched the tape in the secretary's back office," Julia said. "We turned to Chet and asked if it was accurate." Crocker said it was but added that armed actors on both sides were creating a lot of problems.[69]

"That's another issue," Julia said. "This part [the North] they control and they could give us access to it, and I need [Shultz] to say something to the foreign minister." Shultz agreed.[70]

But when the Sudanese foreign minister arrived at the State

Department the next day, he forgot to bring ID, and the clerk at the front desk in the lobby refused to let him in. The Sudanese official grew furious, and a protocol officer was summoned to work it out. By the time the foreign minister arrived in Shultz's seventh-floor office, he was so angry that Shultz never brought up the issue of mass starvation. "We missed that opportunity," Julia said.

Julia contacted the U.S. Embassy in Sudan to ask for its assessment of the humanitarian crisis, but officials there were not particularly helpful either. "They had major flooding of the White Nile and the Blue Nile, and the [USAID] computers had gone down," Julia said. "You know, that's the trouble in disasters. They weren't focused because they had to move out of their offices. There was also a locust invasion at the time. War, floods, locusts…where was Moses when we needed him?"[71]

The Sudanese government was refusing to let any relief officials into southern Sudan to assess the situation, and the State Department would not allow any Americans to cross into the country from Uganda or Kenya to find out for themselves. "We have diplomatic relations with Sudan," an official told Julia. "It's their sovereign territory. We can't be sending people in across the border in the dark of night to find out how bad the famine is."

Julia was not deterred. "I just hired some other people to do it for me since I couldn't go myself," she said in her LOC oral history. "We got the assessments, and then we knew what we wanted to do."

The way that Julia got those assessments is a good illustration of how she learned to deal creatively within the State Department bureaucracy. Julia and Garvelink met with the International Rescue Committee (IRC) and other private relief organizations that were demanding that the U.S. government take action. "Our State colleagues were telling us there was nothing we could do until the displaced crossed the border where they would be cared for as refugees," Garvelink said. "Julia insisted that we had to do something. So we went to talk to [Deputy Secretary of State] Larry Eagleburger."

Julia and Eagleburger worked out an agreement that Garvelink would accompany a team of private relief organizations, led by the IRC, to Kenya. Garvelink would remain there while the other team members went into southern Sudan and conducted an assessment of needs. Based on their findings, Garvelink would agree on a program with the private organizations that OFDA would fund. "We would then inform the Sudan government of our intention to implement a relief program through private U.S. relief agencies," Garvelink said, "but we would not ask the permission of the government of Sudan. So we were violating Sudan sovereignty, sort of." It was a careful and appropriate cover, and Eagleburger approved it.

Around this time, the U.N. secretary-general decided to get involved with southern Sudan by appointing James Grant, the American head of UNICEF, to take the lead. Grant called Julia and asked her to meet with him in New York, but she was on vacation and asked Garvelink to brief Grant about the political and humanitarian issues involved, as well as the OFDA relief efforts that they started a few months before.

"We explained that we were working with NGOs in southern Sudan and had informed the Khartoum government of our activities, though we had not asked the government's permission," Garvelink said. He explained to Grant that they had food convoys entering southern Sudan through northern Kenya and Uganda, that they were planning to initiate food convoys through Ethiopia into the eastern part of southern Sudan, and they had food convoys moving from central Sudan into the South, as well as food barges on the Nile.[72]

That March, Julia joined up with a congressional delegation making a fact-finding trip to southern Sudan. Their mission was to expedite the flow of humanitarian aid into the war zones. "It's a race against time," Julia told a briefing for reporters in Washington before leaving with the delegation. "Everybody wants peace, but peace will be a hollow victory if the people for whom peace is the goal are not alive because we can't deliver the food in time to save them."[73]

The group flew to Wau and El Muglad in southern Sudan, deep in the territory held by the Sudan People's Liberation Army. No planes, other than relief aircraft, had been allowed to land for two years. "Our pilots were understandably nervous," wrote former Representative Mickey Leland of Texas, then chairman of the House Select Committee on Hunger, who led the delegation and contributed an article about the trip to *Ebony* magazine. "They told us we would fly in high, then dive in to land, using a spiraling maneuver to thwart any troops in the bush who might not have gotten the word not to fire on us." The trip confirmed what the delegation already suspected. "People are dying or at risk of dying in numbers that are mindboggling," Leland wrote.[74]

When Julia returned to the United States, she appeared on ABC's "Nightline," and Ted Koppel asked her how food was being used as a weapon in Sudan. "Food is interdicted by both the rebels who have attacked various convoys and impeded the flights of aircraft, and the government of Sudan [which] has not implemented all the technical agreements they said they would," she replied. "I think it's a question of political will. We have to increase our pressure on them."[75]

Several weeks later, the United Nations announced with great fanfare the launch of Operation Lifeline Sudan, a multimillion-dollar system to get 100,000 tons of food supplies to more than 1 million people. The U.N. hired barges to carry food down the Nile Rivers, camels, donkeys, "whatever we could get to go out to the west," Julia said. "We hired a train to take food from one end of the country to the other. It went about 100 feet and stopped, and we had to figure out how to offload it. It was a logistical nightmare. But it worked, and it worked because we started out modestly...and we tried to make it evenly distributed."

Media attention to the issue—newspapers and magazines, but especially television—was critical to getting the U.S. government to focus attention on the issue. "For the whole African famine, if it hadn't come across on television into the living rooms of American people that these folks were all dying, I think it would have been very difficult to galvanize the level of commitment and concern," Julia said in her oral history. "Media is always very helpful to that."

Renee Bafalis credited Julia with understanding the importance of reaching out to the press. "Julia truly understood just how beneficial the media partnership could be to our efforts, not just in Sudan but throughout the world," Bafalis said. "We worked very hard to nurture and maintain open, honest and transparent relationships with the media over the years. If media outlets had correspondents in a country where a crisis was occurring, their coverage could often drive our disaster response by garnering grass-roots public support, which often generated support on Capital Hill. For this reason alone, it was very important for us to work closely with the media to ensure that the issues they were pursuing were in line with our concerns or needs."

Bafalis said that if news organizations didn't have anyone covering an impending crisis that Julia felt needed attention, she would engage them and hope that their coverage would help change the course of events, which it often did. "When it came to alleviating human suffering, Julia never left any stone unturned," Bafalis said. "The media was just one more mechanism she chose to help her reach that goal."

The overall lesson learned from Operation Lifeline Sudan: "This program was designed for emergency lifesaving, and it has gone through many iterations in the last 20 years," Julia said. "Unfortunately, with each iteration, it has been treated as an emergency program. So there was no infrastructure developed, very few complimentary programs for food, agriculture health care, education, nothing that got the population invested in a more permanent solution. In fact, there was always continual displacement.

"One of the challenges we have in the relief community is trying to identify that when you give emergency assistance, are there ways that you build national capacity? Unfortunately, that lesson has not been learned. When I was last there in 2004, they had one road in the South and very few roads in the North. I mean, this is Sudan, the size of the whole eastern United States. It's an immense country with immense potential that has never been tapped."[76]

Twenty-two years after Julia's first trip to southern Sudan, her daughter, Julie, a reproductive health adviser for the International Medical Corps, spent three weeks there supporting primary and secondary health programs. Julie said that the situation continues to be very dismal, with poor infrastructure, a weak health care system and ongoing conflict, mostly along the border with the North. "Long-term development projects have been challenging to secure because donors have been hesitant to invest, given ongoing unrest and uncertainty," she explained. "There was a lot of anticipation for the upcoming referendum, which was part of the 2005 Comprehensive Peace Agreement that gave the South autonomy and the right to self-determination through referendum six years later."

The referendum was held in January 2011. Six months later, the Republic of South Sudan officially split off from the north and became Africa's 54th country. Most of the relief community continues to be on full alert, as it's uncertain how the transition to independence will go, how borders will be defined and how oil revenue is going to be shared. "The hope," said Julie, "is the country will not devolve into war again." She remains committed to improving health conditions for poor populations in South Sudan and elsewhere.

Her mother would be pleased.

CHAPTER 8

THE ARMENIAN EARTHQUAKE

On December 7, 1988, without warning, two jolts from a magnitude 6.9 earthquake leveled cities and towns in the Soviet Union's Republic of Armenia, leaving at least 55,000 people dead and half a million homeless. Soviet President Mikhail Gorbachev was attending a summit in New York when the earthquake struck.

In the Office of Foreign Disaster Assistance, it had been a busy year. In 1988 alone, in addition to the humanitarian crisis in Sudan, disasters included flooding in Bangladesh, which covered an area almost three times the size of New Jersey and left 25 million people homeless; less-publicized floods in the Dominican Republic, India and Niger; displaced people in Burundi; and a locust plague in Ethiopia.[77]

When the Armenian earthquake struck, communication between the Soviet republic and the outside world was virtually cut off. No one knew exactly how extensive the damage was. But when the growing toll became clear, Gorbachev cut short his trip to the United States and left quickly for Armenia to direct the recovery effort himself.[78]

Americans had not done humanitarian work on any sizable scale in the Soviet Union since the end of World War II, and Julia's disaster response team, which she had only recently organized, had little hope that the Soviets would accept an American offer of help. The Soviet desk at the State Department told her not to even bother.[79]

Julia contacted the White House and suggested that President Reagan personally ask Gorbachev if he would accept the U.S. government's assistance with search-and-rescue efforts. Assured that Reagan would convey the offer, Julia returned to the State Department and told her team to start making preparations to leave. "We immediately began looking for a charter aircraft and began assembling search-and-rescue teams," said Bill Garvelink, OFDA's assistant director for response, who was on the team.

They located a Boeing 747 in New York, and it was cheap, but there was a catch. The plane had been leased previously by a rock band and the upper deck had circular beds and mirrors on the ceiling. "We decided it would not be a great way to arrive in Armenia," Garvelink said.[80]

Despite an encouraging nod from the White House, the Soviet desk at the State Department continued to discourage preparations. "We were told in a very condescending way that we would not get visas for a large number of people anytime soon," Garvelink said. "Julia was beginning to boil." She decided to drop in on her old friend Larry Eagleburger, undersecretary of state for political affairs, who agreed to set up a meeting with officials from the Soviet Embassy for 4 p.m. that day in Julia's office. Eagleburger said it was up to her if she wanted to invite anyone from the Soviet desk to attend.

"Julia decided that I would call the Soviet desk at five minutes to 4 and invite them to the meeting," Garvelink said. "They came rushing down to her office and were dumbfounded when the Soviet officials told them they could pick up a blanket visa for the entire team in an hour. They asked that we put each team member's name and date of birth on one page and they would stamp the page and it would be ready by 5 p.m."

A friend visiting Julia's office asked how long it would take to pull everything together. "The first plane will leave immediately," Julia replied. "It's loaded, on the runway and ready to go. You don't think I'd wait to start until after the president signed the order, do you?"[81]

Five hours after Gorbachev agreed to accept American assistance, at 3:30 a.m. on Saturday, December 10, Julia and her team took off on a fully loaded cargo plane from Dulles International Airport. Packed with relief supplies, the plane also carried six American physicians, eight search-and-rescue dogs with their handlers, a shelter specialist, several Armenian-Americans to help translate, three other government relief workers and Julia's OFDA press secretary, Renee Bafalis. Julia had left home so quickly that the only personal gear she brought was her daughter Julie's pink Strawberry Shortcake sleeping bag. It wouldn't be

Julia getting on Aeroflot plane during the Armenian earthquake in December 1988.
Photo courtesy of Taft family.

very warm, but it was all she had.

The night was cold and clear, and as the aircraft banked to the east, climbing over the Taft family farm in Lorton, Virginia, Julia looked out the window and hoped that Will and their three children were asleep.

The flight was not without incident. When the plane landed in Iceland to refuel, airport ground personnel refused to allow the dogs to de-plane. Their handlers had no choice but to spread newspapers in the back of the cabin. "Oh Jeez, it was a mess," Julia said as she recounted the incident years later. When the plane stopped to refuel a second time in Shannon, Ireland, airport officials would not accept U.S. currency from the American pilots to pay for fuel. So Julia handed them her personal credit card. When she saw thousands of dollars charged on the receipt, she whispered to her press aide Renee, "Don't let me forget to call Will to explain this."[82]

During a third refueling stop, in Eastern Europe, the refueling process was taking exceptionally long. Garvelink got off the plane to see what was going on. He found the pilots sweating profusely with their credit cards laid out on a table. The airport managers would not accept them. Julia placed a call to the U.S. Embassy in Moscow, where a senior official told her he would fax a letter to the airport manager, saying the embassy would pay for the fuel. The nervous manager, who did not want to be the one to hold up the first-ever U.S. humanitarian flight to Armenia, quickly agreed.

When the letter arrived, the senior pilot read it and told Julia it didn't mean anything. "Before he finished his sentence," Garvelink said, "Julia cut him off and told him to shut up and get back on the damn airplane so we could refuel and get out of there."[83]

The State Department sent a second relief plane to Yerevan, a C-141 military cargo jet carrying 19 firefighters from Fairfax County, Virginia, and Miami-Dade County, Florida, all trained in search-and-rescue, plus 5,000 pounds of rescue tools and supplies.

Julia and her team landed in Yerevan on Sunday morning, four days after the earthquake hit, and Julia proceeded immediately to see the head of the Armenian Republic to extend condolences from President Reagan. The weary official handed her a map and said they could go anywhere because everything was ruined. "Where is the greatest damage and where can we help most?" Julia asked. He told her that Leninakan, the republic's second-largest city with a population of 290,000, was near the epicenter of the quake and had been nearly devastated.

"OK," Julia said, "we're on our way."

Communication between Leninakan and the rest of the country had been almost totally cut. Bridges and roads suffered extensive damage. There was no electricity, drinkable water or gas. All hospitals in the disaster area were destroyed, and 80 percent of local doctors and other medical personnel were either killed or injured. But the road to the city had been reopened.[84] "It was the silence of the towns that captured for me the nature of the human grief," Julia said afterward in a "Nightline" interview with Ted Koppel. "It was all very quiet, except for the sound of cranes. People were stunned."[85]

By the time the buses carrying the Americans entered the city, night had fallen, and the small team was stunned to see silhouettes of people digging through 20-foot-high piles of rubble that used to be six- and seven- story buildings. Truckloads of black coffins were heading into the city. "My first impression was that this was the aftermath of a major bombing," Julia said later at a news conference in Moscow that I covered for *TIME* magazine. "It was like a war zone. Smoke was thick in the air, and there were people sitting next to piles of rubble that had been their homes, straining to hear the voices of loved ones. Everyone there knew someone or had someone in their family lost."[86] Dr. Gail Anderson, one of the team physicians, then director of the surgery emergency clinic at Atlanta's Grady Memorial Hospital, was equally horrified. "Death and destruction surrounded us in a 360-degree arc," he wrote in an article for the *Atlanta Journal-Constitution*. "I wondered if this was what the aftermath of a nuclear war would look like."[87]

To set up a command post, the Americans located the only building in the city that had not been destroyed. It was two stories high and filled with children's furniture and paintings, suggesting it had been a school. The Soviet secret police had already found the building and moved their headquarters into the first floor. As Julia passed a cluster of KGB tanks outside, she turned to Renee Bafalis and whispered: "I hope to hell they don't know that my husband is the deputy secretary of defense."

The team split into two groups. Julia and some of the relief workers took over a small room on the second floor and began unloading supplies: 1,000 hard hats, 1,000 pairs of work gloves, 20,000 face masks, 30 trauma kits, 12 tents; as well as cots, blankets, hand tools and box after box of MREs—Meals Ready to Eat—consisting of vacuum-sealed bags of spaghetti, stews and even cigarettes, a few of which Julia probably smoked when she thought no one was looking.

The team hauled five heavy rolls of plastic sheeting and four 3,000-gallon water tanks up a narrow, wooden stairway.[88] A Soviet guard, who had never imagined foreign relief workers in his country, yelled, "What are you doing? Who's in charge? Who's the man in charge?"

"I'm in charge," Julia replied, smiling broadly and pulling herself up to her full five feet, ten inches.

"What?" the guard replied, incredulous that a woman—a tall, elegant American woman—could hold such an important position.

"We're from the United States, and we've brought search-and-rescue teams," Julia said. "We've got commodities, and we're here to help."

This time, the guard didn't hesitate. "OK," he said. "Move in."[89]

In late afternoon, Julia went outside with two men to look for additional space to set up tents, and two drunken Armenians wandered over and asked in broken English, "Are you British?"

"No," she replied. "I'm American."

"You're an American?" one man said, stupefied. "What are you doing here?"

"We're here to help," Julia said.

The drunk replied: "But America is our enemy."

"America is not your enemy," Julia said. "We care very much about the people of Armenia."

With that, the drunks started hugging her, and one said: "I lost my mother, I lost my father, I lost my sister, I lost two brothers, they're all gone." The other man, who was holding his friend up, said, "Yes, we have each other, but we don't have anyone else." Then they thanked Julia for coming and staggered off.

That night, Julia found herself sharing the second-floor room with 10 male colleagues who were sleeping in warm, military-issue sleeping bags, snoring away, while she lay awake shivering in her daughter's lightweight, fluffy pink sleeping bag. Julia and Renee Bafalis, who had stuffed herself into her own childhood leopard-print sleeping bag, were the only women in the group. The area was experiencing continuous aftershocks, and they worried the building might collapse. "Holy God, we're never going to survive this," Julia said. They chose a spot near the windowsill because it was the most secure part of the room; still, they couldn't relax. "It was bitter cold, but the smell of death was in the air and only got worse as the days progressed," Bafalis said.[90]

There was no toilet on the second floor, so that night Julia and Renee went outside with a flashlight to relieve themselves. "We couldn't use the KGB's toilet on the first floor because it didn't work and was beyond disgusting," Bafalis said. "We went down the steps, making our way in the dark through the KGB tanks and across the street into what we thought was a little park. We just squatted where we could. I remember tripping in the dark and falling through a casket and onto the body inside it. It was horrifying." The next morning, they saw that what they thought was a park had actually been turned into a dumpsite for the corpses of quake victims, which had been tossed into makeshift wooden coffins, like those they had seen while driving into the city.

Julia marched back into the building where they were staying and told her colleagues, "You know what, you're making us a toilet because I am not going out to that park again to go to the bathroom." Fred Cuny, one of the relief workers, found an empty cardboard packing box, stuffed a large plastic bag in it and added a piece of cardboard for a lid. "And that's what 12 people used for their toilet," Julia said. "I'm telling you, it was pretty raw."[91]

The next day, a Swiss relief team moved out of one of the second-floor rooms and the Americans put their toilet inside. But when they returned to use it, someone had locked the door. So Fred Cuny made another toilet and put it outside the door of their room. But that night it was stolen. "It was just unbelievable," Julia said. "There were dead people all over, and the relief teams were fighting over a toilet."

The firefighters and dog handlers had other concerns. The dogs had to be kept away from the devastation to keep their smelling ability intact. So they all camped in a field at the Leninakan airport opposite two collapsed buildings, sleeping four to a tent, with no heat. Snow fell during the day, and at night, temperatures dipped into the 20s. "For me, one of the hardest things was the cold," said Carlos Castillo, a 28-year-old firefighter from Miami. Castillo managed to change his clothes only once the week he was there. "I waited until midday when the sun was the hottest, and I warmed up by the fire for 30 minutes," he said. "Then I dashed into the tent to change."

Cement dust from the buildings presented another concern. The dog handlers had to keep wiping it from the canines' noses to allow them to smell effectively.[92] "There was a shroud of death and an odor permeating the town that was so melancholy," Julia told Ted Koppel. "It affected everybody."[93]

Of all the problems the team members encountered, communication turned out to be the most frustrating. The hand-held radios they had brought had such limited range that Julia and her group could not communicate with the rescue personnel camped at the airport. "We were just about strangled in our ability to do anything because the radios didn't reach," said Fred Krimgold, an architect on the team who specialized in building in earthquake zones. "We couldn't tell where anyone was."[94]

The Americans also found themselves in the middle of a tense ethnic situation. Armenian nationalists were furious at Moscow and Gorbachev because the Soviet president had rejected their claim to Nagorno-Karabakh, a predominantly Armenian enclave in the neighboring republic of Azerbaijan. For 10 months, the two republics had been locked in a bloody dispute over the territory that cost 60 lives, and Gorbachev had sent troops to restore order.[95]

The earthquake did nothing to abate the tensions. Some Azerbaijanis sent congratulatory cables to their neighbors, and some celebrated the tragedy. "Most of the Armenians we saw hated the Russians and believed they wouldn't help them," Bafalis said.[96]

When local residents realized that the Americans had rescue equipment, they surrounded the building and begged the aid workers to come to their homes to dig out survivors from the rubble. Carlos Castillo, the firefighter, uncovered a woman who had been trapped for seven days in a collapsed apartment building. In her arms, she held the lifeless bodies of two grandchildren.[97]

Fred Krimgold, the architect, spotted the woman, who was wedged between a table and her refrigerator, and he began pulling apart the debris with his hands. But suddenly, one of the firefighters, a former Marine, yanked him away. "Listen," the fireman yelled. "You're the technical expert. We're the guys to do this."

The grandmother's leg was trapped in the rubble. To free her, an American surgeon had no choice but to amputate her leg at the knee.[98] "It took five hours to get her out," Julia said afterward in an interview on PBS's "MacNeil/Lehrer NewsHour." "Her grandchildren's limbs were wrapped around her, and she was trying to hold and comfort them. One of the surgeons had to amputate the leg of one of the children to allow the breathing passages of the woman to be relieved of the pressure."[99]

Despite all their efforts, the American team found only one other survivor. "Most of the people had already died when we got there," Julia said. "But we would go to their homes with the dogs, and the dogs would report that there were no live smells. Then we would end up having to tell the people that there was nothing there. It was so emotional because all we could do was hug them and hand out masks and shovels."

Hundreds of thousands of Armenians were now homeless as a result of the earthquake, making housing a top priority. The Soviets decided to send women and children to temporary housing on the Black Sea, a popular summer spa resort where there were empty rest homes. The men would stay to help rebuild the city. But the American team was opposed to the idea, arguing that Armenian families would be further traumatized by being separated. "Don't do that," Julia scolded Soviet officials. "Let the people stay and help rebuild the city."[100]

At one point, Julia was caught between "the Battle of the Freds." Fred Cuny, a six-foot, five-inch Texan, whose humanitarian relief experience to that point had centered mostly on undeveloped countries, came up with an idea for housing people and animals. A former Marine with a gung-ho personality, Cuny convinced Julia that the Armenians should build sod houses, half above ground, half under ground. "If they didn't protect the cattle and pigs in the winter, they would have a huge problem in the spring," Julia said. "So we gave them a design for sod houses that used plastic sheeting. It was very innovative."[101]

Fred Krimgold, the architect, thought Cuny was nuts. "It was going to be 20-degrees Fahrenheit for four or five more months," Krimgold said. "I told Fred it was ridiculous to convince Julia that these people should stay here in the middle of winter with no supplies, no electricity, no water, no sanitation and no communication, when the country had empty rest homes on the Black Sea. If we had this kind of situation in the United States, we would not be putting people up in tents in the middle of winter.

"Julia thought that Cuny's idea was the American contribution of global experience," Krimgold said, "but it was not. We were not dealing with rural peasants but with people who had rockets, satellites and nuclear missiles. Treating Armenia like the Third World was a big mistake."[102]

In fact, the Soviets liked the idea of sod houses. "They embraced the idea," said Garvelink, "and when I returned to the area several years later, those structures were still there and in use."

This was not the first time "the Freds," as they called themselves, had disagreed. Years earlier, after one of their first relief projects together, Cuny commissioned a potter in Texas to make him two cups. "One of them was Fred Practice," Krimgold said, "and the other was Fred Theory. He was Fred Practice, and I was Fred Theory."[103] Years later, while working in Chechnya during the civil war, Cuny disappeared and was presumed killed. His body was never found.

Renee Bafalis said that one of her primary jobs was to help maintain order among several Armenian-Americans on the team who were outspoken about their dislike for the Soviets. "At one point when we were in Yerevan, I overheard one of the Armenian-Americans talking on an old green pay phone in a little booth in the lobby of the hotel, blasting the Soviet government's response to the earthquake," Bafalis said. She realized he was doing an interview with National Public Radio. "What the hell are you doing?" she yelled. "You're making not only yourself but our team a target. Number 1, the phones are all bugged. Number 2, you're jeopardizing our mission." Then she grabbed the phone out of his hand and hung it up. Nothing more was said.[104]

When the search-and-rescue effort was completed, the Soviets planned to bring in a demolition team to raze the city. The American team was opposed. "Don't do that," Julia told one official. "You can't. You're not going to find people alive after 10 days, but people have to come to closure."

The Americans had no satellite phone, which made it impossible to communicate directly with Washington. And this was long before the age of cell phones and e-mail. "It's unbelievable how unprepared we were," Julia said. The team relied on sending messages to the State Department by relaying information to a team member in Yerevan, who would then place a call to Washington. Julia was eager to get to Moscow, where she could send secure cables back to the State Department from the American Embassy.

While the search-and-rescue team stayed in Leninakan, Julia and Renee found a ride to Yerevan, where they hoped to catch a plane to the Soviet capital. The driver, whom they didn't know, gave the women his calling card and said that if they had any trouble getting a plane seat, they should show his card to Armenian officials. And sure enough, when they arrived at the airport, airline personnel told them that no planes would be flying to Moscow that day.

"Do you still have that card?" Julia asked Renee, who fished it from her backpack and presented it to an Armenian official. Ten minutes later, they were escorted to a plane and told to board. "The plane looked like it was going to fall apart," Julia said, "but at least it was there." They never did determine the source of their driver's clout in the Armenian hierarchy but decided that he had enough of it to get them where they needed to go without question.

Before she left Yerevan, Julia tore up all the notes of recommendations she had written on how the Soviets should proceed with the relief effort. "I had been to the Soviet Union before," she said. "We had been very blunt about what they should and should not do, and I was afraid to carry the notes around. I don't know why I was getting a little paranoid, but after two or three days, they had all these military people with guns guarding against looting. I thought, 'Oh God, I don't need this,' so I tore up the notes and flushed them down a toilet at the airport."

Once on board, the women looked around and were appalled at the condition of the plane. The aisles were filthy, and luggage bins were littered with feathers and excrement from live chickens that had been transported in the overhead bins. "It was falling apart...an unbelievable piece of junk," Bafalis said. "In the States, there is no way that you would get on a plane like this. Julia and I sat there praying the entire trip that we would make it to Moscow without crashing."[105]

Upon arrival, they found a car waiting for them, courtesy of U.S. Ambassador Jack Matlock Jr. They were driven directly to Spaso House, the early 20th-century neoclassical residence of the ambassador, where they spent a much-needed, comfortable night. The next day, Julia held a news conference at which she was asked whether such an extensive, dangerous effort was worthwhile for the American team when only two lives were saved. "The number of lives you save is important," she replied. "But the hope you give to people that you are trying to find their loved ones is also important. If they tell you they hear a voice and you take a dog and find nothing, you can tell them there is no more hope, and they are relieved because they can make the break."[106]

On Julia's trip back to the United States, the plane stopped for a layover in Frankfurt, where she was interviewed by ABC's Koppel for "Nightline" and NBC's Jane Pauley for "Today." "It was the most dramatic experience of my life," Julia told Pauley in a shaky voice. "Being on the scene, witnessing and participating in it were overwhelming. Helping people in their initial grieving process was unspeakably moving."[107]

Julia and Renee arrived back in Washington on December 16, emotionally and physically drained. The next day, Julia went to the White House to brief President Reagan, Vice President George H.W. Bush and Colin Powell, who was Reagan's national security adviser. "I'd known Colin since 1972, so he was already a friend," Julia said. "And I knew Bush because I had accompanied him on a trip to Ecuador, but I didn't really know Reagan. And he was quite impressive.

"I started out saying the earthquake had happened on Pearl Harbor Day and then described the cooperation and responsiveness, and Reagan said, 'This strikes me as a real turning point for Russia. First there was Chernobyl where they found how vulnerable they were to a catastrophe and unable to cope, and now this will further shock their system. I think there will be changes.'"

Bush told Julia that his son and grandson would like to go to Armenia to hand out Christmas presents. She stifled a laugh: "I thought to myself, 'For God's sake, this is not a good idea.' But all I said was, 'When would you go?'"

"The 24th of December," Bush replied.

Unable to contain herself, Julia said: "Their Christmas is January 6th, and between now and then, they have a few other things to do besides worry about your security and accepting gifts."

When the meeting was over, Julia called Powell aside. "Colin, get him off this," she said in a tone considerably more blunt than the one she had used with Bush. "It's ridiculous."

Powell replied, "I can't. They are all tied up in wanting to do this."

So on December 24, Bush's son, Jeb, and grandson, George P. Bush, left for Armenia, carrying more relief supplies and Christmas gifts for earthquake victims." I mean, this was just stupid," Julia said years later in recounting the event. "They didn't even get to the sites that were most affected."

Two days after Julia briefed Reagan, the rest of her search-and-rescue team returned to the United States. "At some point, you have to stop searching," Julia said, adding that sniffer dogs tire after three or four days. "And when there is a heavy stench of death, as in Leninakan, it is hard for them to distinguish odors."[108] Julia and Renee went to Andrews Air Force Base to greet their colleagues, accompanied by two psychologists who specialized in post-traumatic stress disorder. "Julia told us that she knew what a hard time she was having and figured we would all react in similar ways," Bafalis said. "The psychologists spent an hour counseling us about what to expect and how to deal with all we had experienced. Julia was always thinking about the team and what would be best for us. She was the most compassionate person I have ever known and a devoted caregiver to all of us."

Julia's favorite holiday had always been Christmas, but that year was different. "I just couldn't get up for it," she said. "I mean, why would I be buying presents and decorating the houses when I'd just seen these people's lives totally destroyed? I was really very sad. We did have people come in and do some counseling for us at the office and that helped a little bit, but even now, every once in a while, I still get some sadness.

President Ronald Reagan meets disaster rescue workers at the White House in Washington who recently returned from the earthquake in Armenia, Dec. 22, 1988. From left are: Mike Tamillow of Fairfax County, Va.; Foreign Disaster Relief Director Julia Taft; Reagan; Caroline Hebard, a dog team handler from Bernardsville, N.J.; and Doug Jewett of Dade County, Fla. (AP Photo/Barry Thumma)

"For me, this was just a short-term assignment, so you can imagine what people who have had to live through the wars in Iraq are going through. How in the world do you resolve the fact that you have survived and you can do nothing to help? That's why we spent an awful lot of time hugging people. The physical contact was helpful to the survivors, but it was also helpful to us. That was, you know, 16, 17 years ago, and I still have some flashbacks. It's the only time, before or since, that I suffered from post-traumatic stress syndrome."

In 1989, at a ceremony at the Soviet Embassy in Washington, Soviet Ambassador Yuri Dubinin presented Julia Taft and her team with the Supreme Soviet Award for Personal Courage.

CHAPTER 9

WAR IN BOSNIA: 1992-1995

In 1989, President George H.W. Bush named Will Taft as U.S. Permanent Representative to NATO, which carries the rank of ambassador. That August, the family moved to Brussels, where Taft spent much of his time helping the Western alliance focus on the reunification of Germany after the fall of the Berlin Wall and the political transitions of Eastern Europe and the Soviet Union. The family returned to Washington in the summer of 1992.

That fall, Bill Clinton trounced Bush in the presidential election, ending 12 years of Republican control of the Executive Branch. Will Taft left government and joined the private law firm of Fried, Frank, Harris, Shriver & Jacobson. Julia became a consultant for InterAction, an umbrella group for international relief and development agencies, and she would soon lead a coalition of relief organizations to Bosnia, where civil war had broken out and tens of thousands of refugees needed aid.

In fact, the entire region was unraveling. After the former Soviet Union imploded in 1990, people who had lived for decades under communist rule in other countries began trying to overthrow their governments. In 1991, the communist government of Yugoslavia collapsed, and various ethnic factions in the country began fighting each other to gain political power and control of the territory. The country dissolved into new, independent state/countries, including Bosnia and Herzegovina, Serbia, and Croatia.

In March 1992, Bosnia-Herzegovina declared its independence, and Serbs living there took up arms and began a campaign to drive out other ethnic groups and create a purely Serbian territory. Most of the towns in Bosnia-Herzegovina fell, except for Sarajevo, the capital. On April 6, 1992, Serb militants opened fire on thousands of unarmed peace demonstrators gathered outside the Holiday Inn in Sarajevo, smashing windows and setting off grenades inside the hotel.[109] It was the beginning of one of the longest sieges of modern warfare in history. Over four years, 10,000 people died, including an estimated 1,500 children.

Yet even with such human tragedy unfolding, Western nations were reluctant to use military force to halt the Serbian attacks on Muslims and Croats, fearful of getting bogged down in a civil war with no end in sight. "There were U.N. peacekeepers in the region, but the situation was really grim," Julia said. "These airlifts were managed by the U.N., and the only way you could get in and out of the city was via their planes."

By winter, food supplies that had kept 2.3 million Bosnians from starvation were running out, and the Serbs controlled the gas, turning it off and on at will. "We decided we needed to get much more engaged in humanitarian relief," Julia said. "So I joined a group of about five or six other NGO leaders, and we prepared our strategy."

In January 1993, she led a coalition that included other private relief agencies to the Balkans to arrange for providing aid. They planned to go to Croatia and from there to Bosnia and the cities of Mostar and Sarajevo to raise the alarm for thousands of people in the eastern part of Bosnia who had been totally cut off. "We sent ahead people who found the smugglers' routes, the roads used by backpack animals to get food into these far-away villages," Julia said. "But when our teams started getting into these areas, they sent word back that a lot of the villagers were already dead."

Before leaving Washington, Julia talked with Jim Woolsey, who was about to become director of the CIA, and Colin Powell, chairman of the Joint Chiefs of Staff. "I had known both men since we all worked for the Nixon administration," Julia said, "and we were close friends as well as colleagues. I said, 'Listen, I know you don't want to have U.S. troops going in there, but somebody's got to get some aid to these people. I'm going to go over, and I'll come back with as much information as I possibly can. This will help you figure out whether there can be a coordinated U.S. relief effort.' So off I went, headed for Croatia with the group. When we arrived, we were shocked by all the devastation. Oh my God, it was awful."

The Serbs and the Croats, the two largest and most antagonistic groups of the old Yugoslav federation, had been fighting for weeks on Croatia's Adriatic coast, and U.N. peacekeeping troops were caught in the middle. According to the *New York Times*, the fighting raised the possibility that the U.N. troops might withdraw from Croatia, which would open the door to a resumption of full-scale war between the Serbs and Croats. There was also renewed fighting between Croats and Muslims and Serbs and Muslims in neighboring Bosnia.[110]

Julia flew into the city of Zagreb by commercial airline. "The relief situation was quite bad because there were so many displaced persons," she said. "They were not refugees because they were not technically out of their country, but they were in holding sites, and the conditions were unbelievable."

The group flew to the city of Split in southern Croatia, where they found more displaced persons camps, filled with Croats and Bosnians. Then they drove into Mostar, an ancient city famous for the Stari Most, a stone arch bridge commissioned by Suleiman the Magnificent, the sultan then reigning over the Ottoman Empire, and completed in 1566.

The city, with a mixed population of Bosnians and Croats, was situated in a valley surrounded by the high mountains of Herzegovina. "Mostar was so striking because you could so clearly see the divisions," Julia said. "In the cemeteries, everyone had their special *nilas* (headstones) the Bosnians had theirs, the Croats had theirs. It was such a striking portrayal of the divisiveness of this society."

When they arrived, Julia told the group that they were going to cross the old bridge to the Muslim side of the river to ask the people what their needs were. "No way," one of the group members replied. "We are not going on this bridge. It's going to be blown up."

"OK," Julia told me. "There *was* active fighting. But we had come all this way, and I was determined to go." She told the group that the bridge had been around for hundreds of years and that the country had such a strong sense of culture that no one would ever blow it up. Julia started walking across the bridge and turned around. "Guess what?" she said in recounting the story. "The other seven people were timidly following me." They found that the Muslims living on the other side of the river had been totally cut off from assistance because relief workers were afraid to cross the bridge.

The next month, a U.N. relief worker was killed in a shelling attack on convoys taking the same overland supply route from Mostar to Sarajevo. And less than a year later, in November 1993, the bridge *was* shelled and collapsed into the river. "The damned thing was blown up by Bosnian Croats," Julia said.

When Julia announced that the next stop was Sarajevo, the group objected again. Julia prevailed. "We've come all this way," she said. "We've got to use those smugglers' maps and find out what is really going on there."

They flew into the mountain-ringed city by military aircraft. The pilots told the group that when they landed, they would not turn off the plane's engines. "They would stop, open the back of the plane, and we'd jump off," Julia said. "They would close it up and take off again. They told us to run across the tarmac and get into the SUV, which is what we did." A caravan of armored SUVs drove Julia's team into the city.

They arrived at the only functioning hotel, a Holiday Inn. Its top floors had been blown off in fighting months before, but it did have rooms available, as well as a dining room that served one Spartan meal a day. As Julia tells the story, the group entered the huge lobby, which had smashed windows, chandeliers dangling from the ceiling and light fixtures lit only with candles. "Two guys that are with me, they went up to the front desk in front of me and said they wanted a double room 'on the safe side.' The hotel clerk assigned them to room No.102."

Julia was next. "I'd like to have a room on the safe side, please," she said.

"We have only one room left," the clerk replied. "It's No. 523."

"That doesn't sound like the safe side, if room No. 102 is on the safe side," Julia replied. "Am I on Sniper Alley?" She was referring to the boulevard in front of the hotel where people often had to dodge gunfire.

"Yes," the clerk said.

When Julia got to her fifth-floor room, she found taped-over windows that had been shattered by gunfire. "And yes," she said, "it looked out over Sniper Alley. There were buildings across the street where gunshots were fired all the time. I looked behind my bed and the whole back of the wall had been gouged out by machine gun fire." Julia stood there for a moment in disbelief. "Oh great," she muttered to herself. Then she put her bags down and went to find someone to lead her to the International Rescue Committee. But, in her words, "there were no taxis, no buses, no nothing."

At the front desk, Julia found a driver for an armed convoy. "Would you mind giving me a lift?" she asked. "I've got an address." The location turned out to be a house on a hill, near the hospital. "All throughout the drive, I could see diversionary blockades that people could hide behind if there was shooting," Julia said. "The driver was a madman. He was all over the place.

"We got there, and he let me off. I walked up to the door and knocked and knocked and rang and rang, but nobody answered. I thought, 'This is great. I'm in the middle of nowhere.' Finally, somebody came out. It was my friend Lionel Rosenblatt, then president of Refugees International, who was key to the humanitarian effort. We talked about how we needed to get more specifics about deaths, casualties, displaced persons and about the conditions in the eastern part of the country."

Rosenblatt had arrived in Sarajevo a few weeks earlier. Philanthropist George Soros had made a $50 million donation to the U.N. Refugee Agency (UNHCR) to provide humanitarian aid to Bosnia and asked Refugees International for advice on how the funds could be best used to help victims of war. "Those were dark times," Rosenblatt said. "It was the first winter of the siege, and morale was at a low point. We even talked about how we would evacuate Sarajevo if we had to." That New Year's Eve, Rosenblatt had facilitated entry into Sarajevo for veteran diplomat Richard C. Holbrooke, then ambassador to Germany. "When Holbrooke left, he was deeply committed to saving Sarajevo and ending the war in Bosnia," Rosenblatt said. "This was an epiphany for him." Holbrooke, who would become architect of the Dayton Peace Accords that eventually ended the war in Bosnia, began lobbying for greater force to be used against the Serbs, including U.S. and NATO airpower.[111]

After meeting with Rosenblatt, Julia returned to the Holiday Inn. The weather was bitter cold. The hotel had no electricity or running water. And she still had the room facing Sniper Alley: "I thought, 'This is it, curtains, my last night on Earth,'" Julia said. "So I wrote a letter to my husband and kids saying, basically, 'This is it, babes. I'm not going to live through this.'" (Julia told me that she still had the letter, but I never found it.)

She grabbed her Kevlar vest, her helmet and a blanket and went into the bathroom: "I crawled into the bathtub and thought, 'Now I have an extra wall between me and Sniper Alley. This is the safest place I am going to be. But after about two hours, I thought, 'Julia, if this is your last night on Earth, why are you trying to sleep in this stupid tub when it is so uncomfortable? Go sleep in the bed.' So I went over to the bed and piled up a desk and other things between it and the window so that I would have a little bit more barrier. It was hysterical."

The next morning, she was picked up in a car that took her to the Sarajevo hospital. "The driver ran in with some medicines," Julia said. "He got back in the car, drove down the hill, which took all of 30 seconds, turned the corner, and we heard a huge explosion. A 120-millimeter explosive round hit exactly where our car had been—exactly." Shaken, they took off quickly for the presidency building, which was where Refugees International had its headquarters. Here Julia met up again with Lionel Rosenblatt, who gave her smugglers' maps, data on the number of people killed and displaced and those who still needed help. He probably helped settle her nerves as well. "He was a real hero," Julia said.

Rosenblatt said they talked about how to help people in the outlying areas of the region who had been completely cut off and needed assistance. They also discussed the possibility of engaging the Russians to help provide assistance to eastern Bosnia. "Julia and I were passionate about helping people who were cut off," Rosenblatt said.[112]

Julia returned to Washington and started lobbying Colin Powell, Jim Woolsey and others. "General John Shalikashvili [then NATO supreme commander] was one of those trying to develop a joint plan with Russia to get access to this area," Julia said. "And Shali was very supportive, but Colin was not."

Julia argued with Powell. "Colin said it would take 200,000 people, and I said, 'Colin, it won't take 200,000 people,'" she said. "'What you can do is joint patrols, decide who is going to do bridges, things like that. This is a time that [our relations] were pretty good with Russia.' And he said, 'Nope, 200,000 people, we're not doing it.' I was really disappointed in him. But I came back and did all the proper debriefings, and then I sent Jim [Woolsey] all of the smugglers' maps so that maybe some of his CIA people could get in. But we really blew it; we never focused on the eastern part of the country, which was an area that was not in contention by any of the other powers around. It could have actually been a very collaborative effort. And to this day I regret that."

To help areas that had been cut off from assistance, private relief agencies came up with some creative strategies. They started small businesses that the refugees could run themselves. "Instead of importing relief supplies, we showed them how to make up beds, how to make blankets," Julia said. "All too often in our business, we send in materials and forget that there is a local economy that local people can use. The way we operated in Bosnia was very effective."

There were, needless to say, many private and U.S. government-funded programs operating in the Balkans during these years. Julia was hardly alone. But she was always a standout, a commanding presence with a fine-tuned sense of how to rally people around the causes closest to her heart.

"Julia was a catalyst," said Timothy Knight, former OFDA assistant director, who worked with Julia for more than three years and remained a close friend and colleague. "She had the ability to contact influential people and engage them. And like a catalyst, she brought attention to an event so everyone could and would work better together. The International Rescue Committee, the Catholic Relief Services and lots of other organizations were there, but Julia's focus improved their standing by calling attention to the situation and creating more resources for everyone."[113]

CHAPTER 10

INTERACTION: "HERDING CATS"

In May 1993, Julia was asked to be CEO of InterAction, a coalition of international relief and development agencies. At first, she resisted the appointment. "I'm just too disorganized and too bossy for this type of job," she said.

But Julia's political skills were exactly what the young organization needed. "In five years, she turned InterAction into an important advocacy voice, proving once again that she could herd cats," said then-Refugee International President Ken Bacon.[114]

Suzanne Kindervatter, vice president of InterAction, said that when Julia joined the organization, she found herself once again in a world dominated by male leaders. "In the mid-1990s, the biggest international NGOs were all headed by men," said Kindervatter, a longtime close colleague of Julia's. "But with her force of personality and a strategic sense of how Washington operated, she put InterAction on the map politically."

Kindervatter said that Julia knew how to use her political connections to speak out on behalf of refugees and those in conflict situations: "These people were always in her heart and mind, and she could bring them into a room in a way that others could not. She had high-level connections, and she used them to help the people overseas she cared about."

Carolyn M. Long, InterAction's vice president during Julia's tenure at the organization, put it this way: "Julia saw herself as an equal to everyone she encountered, and she would just put her views out there.

She wasn't intimidated by anyone, and people respected that. When Julia entered a room, people stood up and took notice."

One of the first tests Julia faced at InterAction was the inadequacy of the humanitarian aid response to the crisis in the small East African nation of Rwanda in April 1994, when an estimated 800,000 people were slaughtered in the space of 100 days. It was the culmination of brutal ethnic fighting between the country's two rival ethnic groups, the minority Tutsis, considered the aristocracy of the country, and the Hutu regime, peasants who made up 90 percent of the population. The genocide was sparked after a plane carrying the Rwandan president, a Hutu, was shot down as it returned to Rwanda after several peace meetings with Tutsi rebels. The president of Burundi was on the plane, and he also died.

Violence broke out immediately, resulting in Hutu militia indiscriminately killing Tutsi civilians. The United Nations Security Council, dominated by the United States, refrained from labeling the mass murders as genocide so the U.N. would not have to intervene. In effect, the Clinton administration did not want a repeat of the 1993 humiliation in Somalia when American soldiers intervened to save lives; the bodies of several of the soldiers ended up dragged through the streets. In Rwanda, Western nations not only failed to help hundreds of thousands of people but didn't even speak out against the slaughter.[115]

"Fifty thousand people died after they crossed the border into Zaire," said Jim Bishop, a U.S. foreign service officer for more than three decades who served as ambassador to Niger, Liberia and Somalia before joining InterAction to head its disaster response team.

When the Rwanda crisis turned from genocide to refugee relief, money began pouring into humanitarian organizations. Nearly $100 million in cash and goods was given to charitable organizations working in Rwanda, Julia told the *New York Times*. But the *Times* and others began raising questions about how much of that money was actually spent on direct help for refugees. "The people who went to Zaire did not lack compassion and enthusiasm," wrote *Times* reporter Raymond Bonner. "What they did lack was the experience and skills needed to cope with an emergency in Africa, and too often the charities sent what they thought was needed without consulting the experts on the scene."[116]

Bishop said that largely as a result of the Rwanda crisis, Julia encouraged InterAction to participate in the creation of the Sphere

Project, a pioneering initiative put together in 1997 by a consortium of nongovernmental organizations known as the Steering Committee for Humanitarian Response, which defined minimum standards to be met when providing the basic services required in a disaster response and thereby improve their accountability, performance and professionalism. The Sphere Project also formed a humanitarian charter, which shifted the ethical basis for disaster response from charity to human rights. "It was the idea that you don't throw food off a truck and watch people scramble for it, but you provide a method of distribution that respects their human dignity," said Bishop, a founding member of the Sphere management team. "This ensures that aid goes to those most in need instead of the strongest."[117]

Within InterAction, Julia created a management committee to help with organization and started media and advocacy campaigns to educate the public and Congress on the need for greater funding for economic development and humanitarian assistance. "With Julia's leadership and all her know-how about how Washington really works, InterAction began to take its place as a serious advocate for development and humanitarian issues," Carolyn Long said. Over 10 years, InterAction's staff doubled from 25 to 50.[118]

Yet Julia's tenure at InterAction was not without problems. With so many relief agencies within the coalition competing for the same limited pot of U.S. government money, tensions sometimes arose among board members determined to protect their own refugee assistance turf. "Some thought of themselves as God's angels and felt that Julia was not giving them enough attention," Bishop said. "Others thought she had too high a profile, and a high profile often attracted money. They didn't want to be in her shadow."

Julia was sensitive to the need to promote InterAction's members and to put them in the forefront of advocacy efforts. She had member CEOs sign letters to the White House and speak at major forums and at meetings with key government officials. But as a woman with such a commanding presence, she often found herself in the spotlight.

Asked to describe Julia's biggest contribution to InterAction, Bishop replied, "Passion. She was passionate about her work with the organization, and she was passionate about the humanitarian response in disasters. She may have looked and sounded like a WASP, but she had the passion of her Sicilian ancestry."[119]

In September 1995, Julia was selected to be part of the U.S. delegation to the U.N. Fourth World Conference on Women. This conference was being held in Beijing, and delegation seats were highly prized. The honorary chair of the conference was first lady Hillary Rodham Clinton, and most of the U.S. delegation, which was led by U.N. Ambassador Madeleine K. Albright, were prominent Democrats. With all her Republican ties, Julia was surprised and pleased to be invited.

"The delegation provided a new opportunity for Julia to focus explicitly on women within the broader humanitarian and development frame, " said Kindervatter, who went to Beijing as well as part of the NGO team. "It was also the time she broadened her contacts into a network of high-level Democrats. The delegation was a strongly committed feminist group, and the members became quite close. Hillary Clinton and Madeleine Albright didn't know Julia before Beijing, but they sure did afterwards."[120]

There was another aspect of the Beijing conference that was important to Julia. She took Julie, who was just 15. While Julia attended briefings—she had sprained her ankle before the trip and was hobbling on crutches—Julie participated in workshops and presentations put on by NGOs from all over the world.

The "NGO Forum" is a parallel event to the intergovernmental U.N. women's meetings, and the 1995 NGO Forum attracted more than 10,000 participants, a record. The forum was to have taken place in Beijing, but because Chinese officials were concerned about the impact of the large numbers of women from around the world, they banished the forum to the small town of Huairou, about 45 minutes by bus from the capital. After a series of rainy days, the U.S. delegation arrived in Huairou. "I'll never forget watching Julia slouching on crutches through a sea of mud behind Hillary Clinton and Madeleine Albright as they went off to address the forum," Kindervatter recalled years later.[121]

Young Julie Taft also had the opportunity to meet Hillary Clinton, who made headlines with a bold address that cataloged a devastating list of abuses afflicting women around the world and criticized China for limiting free discussion of women's issues at the conference. "It is time for us to say here in Beijing, and the world to hear, that it is no longer acceptable to discuss women's rights as separate from human rights," the first lady said to cheers and tears from a wildly receptive audience.

"It is a violation of human rights when babies are denied food, or drowned, or suffocated, or their spines broken, simply because they are born girls," Mrs. Clinton said, or "when women and girls are sold into slavery or prostitution for human greed.

"It is a violation of human rights when women are doused with gasoline, set on fire and burned to death because their marriage dowries are deemed too small," she continued, or "when thousands of women are raped in their own communities and when thousands of women are subjected to rape as a tactic or prize of war."[122]

Julie was thrilled to witness such an important conference. "There weren't many kids there, and everyone was excited that Mom had brought her daughter," Julie said.[123]

Two years later, Julia arranged for Julie, by then 17, to spend six weeks doing volunteer work in a Liberian refugee camp on the western border of Ivory Coast. Julia took Julie there herself and made the trip into an adventure. They landed in Abidjan, the commercial capital of Ivory Coast, and spent a few days visiting markets to buy beads and fabrics, eating in cafes and strolling on the beaches. Then they took an uncomfortable, eight-hour drive to Rainbow Camp in the dusty town of Guiglo. The refugee camp had no computers, so Julie took one as a donation for allowing her to work there.

"My first assignment was to set up the long-awaited computer that I had brought with me from the U.S.," Julie said. "Everyone was very excited about its arrival, and I followed the instructions carefully to make sure it was done correctly. After a final rundown of the checklist, everything looked to be in place, so I took the plug and inserted it into the wall. A loud pop and a spark flew from the outlet. I had fried the computer with 220 volts, not realizing I needed to attach the adapter! I was immediately taken off of IT duties." For the rest of her stay, Julie's assignment was to color in pictures that were used to promote good health behavior, as well as to participate in community performances that taught the importance of hand washing, latrine use and personal hygiene.

During the fourth week of her stay, Julie came down with amoebic dysentery and spiked a fever of 107 degrees. Because there was no phone or Internet in Guiglo, Julie was unable to communicate with her parents. She spent the last two weeks of her visit recovering. Her final memory of the trip was the long drive back to Abidjan, where she would catch a flight for home.

About an hour into the ride, she saw a man on the side of the road holding a large rodent by its tail, measuring about two feet long. "My heart stopped as the driver began to slow down and pull over to the side of the road," Julie said. "After he negotiated a price he was satisfied with, he put the rodent on the seat next to me, got back in the car and we continued our journey. For seven hours, on extremely rough roads, I sat next to a 20-pound bush rat with a bashed-in head and flailing limbs. Every time we hit a bump, I gasped. Somehow this final road trip in Ivory Coast marked only the beginning of what I hope will be a long journey in the field."

Julia had set the groundwork for Julie to follow in her footsteps.

CHAPTER 11

REFUGEE CRISIS IN KOSOVO

Julia's participation in the women's conference in Beijing acted as another career springboard. Her commitment to refugee issues had impressed many of the Democratic women on the U.S. delegation, including Madeleine Albright. When President Clinton was re-elected in November 1996, he chose Albright to be his secretary of state, largely at the urging of first lady Hillary Clinton. In September 1997, Clinton issued a press release from his vacation retreat in Martha's Vineyard naming Julia Taft to be assistant secretary of state for population, refugees and migration.

For the second time in her life, Julia would be working for a Democratic administration. (She worked on drug abuse policy in the Carter White House under drug czar Peter Bourne.) Bill Clinton needed a seasoned humanitarian aid expert because all hell was breaking out again in Eastern Europe.

The Dayton Peace Accords, brokered in October 1995 by special envoy to the Balkans Richard C. Holbrooke, paved the way for ending years of ethnic warfare. The agreement established relative peace in the area by creating two new entities, the Serb Republic and the Federation of Bosnia and Herzegovina, each within the sovereign state of Bosnia and Herzegovina. In hopes of ending further ethnic conflicts, Muslims and Croats would control one part of the country, Bosnian Serbs the other. It was considered a remarkable accomplishment that many thought should have earned Holbrooke a Nobel Peace Prize.

But the accord failed to bring a lasting peace.

Julia Taft speaks at a news conference in Pristina, Kosovo, on Sunday, November 1, 1998, after touring the restive Serbian province and meeting with relief officials. (AP PHOTO/ Darko Vojinovic)

In February 1998, Serbian leader Slobodan Milosevic unleashed a brutal, three-month campaign of genocide against ethnic Albanian Muslims in Kosovo, severely threatening the credibility of the NATO alliance and virtually ensuring thousands of Albanians a long winter of suffering and starvation. "It was leading up to what could have been a massive humanitarian crisis," Julia said.

Milosevic's forces had systematically destroyed the Albanians' food supplies, killing livestock, as well as burning haystacks and fields. "They were stranded up there with very little access to any kind of shelter or food," Julia said.[124] The United Nations estimated that 265,000 people were homeless.

President Clinton and the NATO alliance had severely underestimated the will and strength of the Serbs and had allowed them to continue unchallenged. Western leaders were under considerable pressure to use air power to stop Milosevic but continued to waver.[125]

One day in late August 1998, Julia was relaxing at the Taft farm in Virginia when Holbrooke called. "Why aren't you in Kosovo?" he asked. "We need your voice." Three days later, Julia was on her way. She toured the region for three days and was shocked at what she found. "It was one of the most heart wrenching-experiences I have had in 25 years working in humanitarian relief," she said at a news conference in Belgrade. "We have a catastrophe looming, and we only have as a world humanitarian community six weeks to help the government of Serbia respond to the crisis. The snows come early, I understand, to this part of the world. With the snow may come the death of many of the more than 300,000 who have been displaced from their homes because of the conflict in Kosovo."[126]

More than 212 villages had been burned, and 50,000 people were living without shelter in the cold and rain of the region's most rugged mountains. The Serbs' strategy, Julia told the *New York Times*, "seems to be the aggressive displacement of civilians and then, when winter comes, saying to the West you can have access and feed them."[127]

Julia was angry that relief efforts of the Western nations lacked a sense of urgency. "It was hard to figure out how to galvanize attention," she told me. "We didn't have dying bodies or anything like that. But throughout the discussions, people always said, 'Well, you know it starts snowing about October 15. And if we don't get them down from the hills, they're going to freeze.' So I glommed onto that idea and sent a cable to the State Department saying that we had to have a massive effort to get these people down from the hills by October 15. This was around September 1, and I laid out a strategy for how to do this."

Julia placed a call to General Wes Clark, the NATO supreme commander whom she had known from his days as a White House Fellow in 1975. She told Clark she needed to transport refugees and asked if he could supply her with a caravan of SUVs. Clark said he didn't think he could get cars but that he could send Humvees. "I said,

'You know, my idea would be that if we could get some Humvees that were identified as Western relief, people would see them and feel safe about coming down from the mountains.' I told him that I wanted pink Humvees to distinguish them from military camouflage." Clark said he would try, and he was good to his word. He supplied Julia with a convoy of Hummers with fluorescent, day-glo orange panels. "I went back in October, and there were orange Humvees all over the place," Julia said.

In an interview, Clark said that he found Julia easier to work with than many humanitarian aid workers because she was a pragmatic problem solver. "She wasn't dogmatic," he said. "Humanitarian aid workers are often afraid of being associated with the military. There's a certain degree of threat that comes to them with the association. They can be mistaken for combatants. But Julia never evidenced any of that. She was much easier to work with than most."[128]

President Clinton was under pressure to marshal American diplomatic and military resources to persuade Milosevic to stop terrorizing Kosovo's ethnic Albanian population. "This humanitarian disaster cannot be ended without a political solution," the *Washington Post* wrote in an editorial, "and a political solution is impossible without a U.S. resolve to use force, if necessary, against Mr. Milosevic's marauding soldiers. President Clinton and his team have promised again and again to show such resolve, but their threats have proved empty. Instead, Mr. Clinton sends his emissaries, again and again, to plead with the war criminal to stop his crimes. Mr. Milosevic has learned he can defy them at no cost."[129]

When Madeleine Albright was Clinton's ambassador to the U.N., she was an early advocate for using force in Bosnia. Now secretary of state, Albright, like Richard Holbrooke, argued for military force against the Serbs. "We are not going to stand by and watch Serbian authorities do in Kosovo what they can no longer get away with in Bosnia," she said.[130]

The refugee situation was getting worse and threatened to destabilize the entire region. That fall, 25,000 to 35,000 Albanian refugees crossed into Montenegro, the smaller and poorer of the two republics that formed the federation of Yugoslavia. Many of the refugees reported being beaten by Serbian border guards.

With high unemployment and its own economy in tatters, Montenegro was in no position to offer much assistance. The United

Julia Taft (left), US Assistant Secretary of State for Population, Refugees and Migration listens as unidentified ethnic Albanian man points towards damaged buildings in the village of Veliki Drenovac (20 kilometers west of Pristina) Thursday Aug. 27 1998. The village was shelled by Serb government forces during the offensive that started last weekend. (AP Photo/POOL/Vadim Ghirda)

States provided funds for food and such supplies as shoes and coats, but the supplies arrived late and not nearly in the quantities needed. After visiting Montenegro that November, Julia expressed her displeasure to the *Washington Post* that "the pipeline was not as well-organized" as it was in Kosovo. "They really need to get focused on this," she said.[131]

The pressure was building for NATO and the United States to form a coalition and force Serbia to pull back. On March 24, 1999, NATO began a relentless bombing of Yugoslav targets that lasted for 11 weeks, driving Serbian forces from Kosovo and stopping Milosevic from persecuting the ethnic Albanian population.[132] "Poor Wes had to bomb the same damn places again and again because every single target had to be agreed on by all of NATO," Julia said. "He had such a terrible time of that. We had, like, 78 days of bombing. And as a result, there were refugees that poured into Albania and tried to get into Macedonia. With the U.N. and other NGOs, we set up facilities to receive these people in Albania."[133]

That April, Julia joined up with Deputy Secretary of State Strobe

Talbott, who was traveling to Macedonia to try to persuade the fragile government not to close its borders to the 200,000 Kosovo Albanian refugees flooding into the country. Thousands more lined up at border crossings to leave Yugoslavia. "We were supposed to go from Albania back to Italy and then to Greece and Macedonia," Julia said. "But we got this urgent call from [U.S. Ambassador to Macedonia] Chris Hill saying we had to get to Skopje immediately."

Two weeks earlier, demonstrators had overrun the American Embassy in Skopje and burned its vehicles. "The Macedonian government was a reluctant partner in the war on Kosovo, and we had strong indications that they were just going to shut down the border, which would have meant tens of thousands of refugees stacked up on the Kosovo side," Hill said in an interview. "So I felt it important to get our team into Skopje and try to negotiate something."

Julia and Talbott left Albania without their suitcases, jumped on a C-123 cargo plane and flew directly to the Macedonian capital. The twin-prop aircraft had been scanned or "painted" by Serb radar, which suggested they might be fired on. To avoid being hit, the pilot took evasive action by gyrating around in the sky and firing off flares and chaff. "The loadmaster in the cargo hold with us, a seasoned professional who was clearly scared shitless, threw up," Talbott said. "The flares scared us as much as the movement because we landlubbers thought they might be enemy missiles." The loadmaster turned absolutely gray. Strobe watched Julia cross herself. "I didn't know you were Catholic," he said.

By Talbott's account, the only person in the cargo hold who was not terrified was Air Force General Robert H. "Doc" Foglesong, a member of Talbott's interagency team on Kosovo: "He was totally cool and helped cool Julia down, saying that he knew from the outset that we were taking evasive action as a precaution and were not necessarily under attack."[134]

Hill was waiting at the airport that night when the group arrived. "They were all pretty shook up," he said.

They drove immediately to Hill's ambassadorial residence, where Hill and Talbott met in the library with the Macedonian prime minister, while Julia consulted in the parlor with U.N. officials and Knut Vollebaek, the foreign minister of Norway, there in his capacity as chairman of the Organization for Security and Co-operation in Europe. "The Macedonians were concerned that the refugee camps would become permanent, like Palestinian refugee camps," Hill said. "We were selling them on the idea that they would be transit camps."

Julia and Strobe began talking with Vollebaek about how to initiate a NATO settlement plan to deal with the refugees. "If you'll commit to taking some, we'll commit to taking some," Julia said.

"Absolutely," Vollebaek replied, "we'll take 5,000."

"Oh wonderful," Julia said, "we'll take 10 [thousand]."

To underscore the point that they did not plan a permanent camp, Vollebaek offered to fly a planeload of 100 refugees to Norway immediately. Then Julia persuaded the U.S. military to give $1 million to the British military to buy tents and build latrines.

After spending the night in a government villa up the street from the American Embassy, Julia and Strobe met with embassy personnel. Because of their quick departure from Albania, they had arrived in Skopje without as much a change of clothes. "I feel very close to Embassy Skopje," Strobe told the staff, "because I am wearing Ambassador Hill's socks."

That day, Julia traveled to Blace, a refugee camp on the Macedonia border, where 60,000 to 70,000 refugees were living in squalid conditions. The embassy was worried about security in the area and had no intention of letting Ambassador Hill accompany Julia. But she was undeterred.

"It was one of the most exciting days of my life," Julia told me. "The refugees had no food, no water; it was raining; it was mucky. They were all there, huddling together, as far as the eye could see." Standing knee-deep in mud, Julia spoke directly with the refugees. "We're working on a plan," she said. "We're going to try to get you all to secure facilities. Just keep the faith."

When Julia returned to the embassy, Hill asked her how the situation compared to refugee camps she had seen in Africa. "She responded by saying that the situation was terrible and she didn't want anyone to think otherwise," Hill said. "But then she described a scene in Sierra Leone, where they were cutting off people's arms and legs and throwing them into piles, and she pulled a healthy baby out of one of these piles."

Julia looked at Hill and said, "I don't mean to minimize this, but one does have to put these things in perspective."

Hill's assessment of Julia Taft: "She was pretty cool."[135]

Lesson learned? "The lesson," Julia told me in an interview, "is that

First lady Hillary Rodham Clinton gestures as she speaks to the media in New York City on Monday, April 19, 1999, at the United States Mission to the United Nations after a meeting of various foundations organizing relief to Kosovo refugees. Behind her is Julia Taft, who recently returned from a fact-finding trip to the Balkans. (AP Photo/Shawn Baldwin)

you have to be able to quantify a need, target a population and provide data to be able to get enough political support for an action plan. If you just say, 'Well, these people are going to be in trouble in the fall,' nothing is going to happen. You have to be very specific about that. And on the side of the refugee resettlement out of Macedonia, I think the key there was the international cooperation, and a lot of that had to do with the network of the people we know."

Julia smiled as she recalled the mission. "Strobe and I had absolutely no authority to bargain with Norway and say if you take 5 or 7 [thousand], we'll take 10-15 [thousand]," she said. "We just said we would do it, and we did. There was nothing from the president or anyone else to say we could do it. We were just doing this on a whim.

"You can be very creative in government to make things work if you don't worry about getting in trouble or if you are a risk taker. If you are a risk taker, you'll do these things. We had a great time."[136]

CHAPTER 12

THE UNITED NATIONS: AFGHANISTAN

When George W. Bush narrowly defeated Al Gore in the November 2000 presidential election, Julia hoped to either keep her State Department job or land another plum—maybe director of the Peace Corps. Julia was, after all, one of the most accomplished and recognized women in her field, a Taft Republican eager to be part of a new Republican administration. And Bush had named her old friend, Colin Powell, to be his secretary of state. In theory, Powell could become Julia's new boss.

But Powell surprised everyone and did not reappoint Julia to the job. He told her, according to friends, that her appointment could not get through the newly conservative White House. Julia may have been a Republican, but in terms of social policy, she had the heart of a liberal, and—by working for the Clinton administration—she had crossed to the enemy camp. Julia felt that she had been stabbed. She told friends that she was "radioactive."[137]

Powell tapped Will Taft to become the State Department's chief legal adviser. (He would eventually become radioactive to the Bush administration as well!)

When Julia left the State Department, Mark Malloch-Brown, a British diplomat who had worked at the World Bank and had recently been appointed administrator of the United Nations Development Programme, asked Julia to join him at the UNDP. That November, U.N. Secretary-General Kofi Annan named Julia director of the UNDP's Bureau for Crisis Prevention and Recovery. Her main responsibility was to head the U.N. task force coordinating the recovery effort for

Afghanistan after the fall of the Taliban government. "UNDP's crisis work was a leisurely and academic affair, a rather casual adjunct to our long term development work," Malloch-Brown said. "I wanted it transformed into a hands on operational capacity, able to plunge in when a country was failing because of war or natural disaster, and help our colleagues on the ground respond effectively. Julia was perfect for the task. UNDP initially did not know what had hit them, but she set about winning them over with her usual irresistible mixture of charm and steel. She had an enormous impact."[138]

Julia moved to New York, found an apartment on East 47th Street and wasted no time getting started. In December, she flew to Berlin to attend a finance meeting of the Afghanistan Support Group, whose goal was to raise Western aid for the reconstruction of Afghanistan. Julia had been on a similar commission when she worked for the State Department, so she already knew the players and the issues.

"I've only been in this job for two weeks," she told the Berlin group, "but I know you, and you know you can trust me. What I'd like to do is set up a quick disbursing fund to fill the needs of government because they have no money, no buildings, no nothing. If you help me establish this donor fund, then we will be able to move very quickly."

A former colleague of Julia's from the Netherlands left the room and placed a phone call. "The Hague will be the first donor," the woman said when she returned. "We'll give one million dollars." After that, said Julia, "it was kind of like a poker game with everybody anteing up." By the end of the day, they had enough money to start the trust fund.

Then they had to decide how to spend it. A new Afghan Cabinet was to begin work in a month, but most buildings in Kabul had been destroyed, and there was no place to meet. Julia called her New York office and asked that the U.N. set up instant offices with satellite phones, faxes, computers and desks. Her team ordered them from Scandinavia so they would arrive quickly. Buildings needed renovation. Each of the 30 Cabinet ministers would be provided not only with an office but also with a car.

An international donors' conference was to be held in Japan on January 21, and the Afghan leader, Hamid Karzai, said that he would like to announce that for the first time in many months, Afghan civil servants would be paid.

"OK," Julia said, "let's figure out how many people there are and how much they ought to be getting, and we'll set up a system of disbursement with the government." The first month's total payroll was $6 million.

"The problem," Julia told me, "was there was no money in Afghanistan, no banks in Afghanistan, no safes in Afghanistan, and there was no way to transfer money." Julia placed a call to U.N. colleagues in Denmark and told them that she needed $6 million in $20 bills flown to Kabul by January 20. But Denmark didn't have it. Then Julia asked that the funds be transferred from a bank in the United States. But no U.S. bank could get the money to Afghanistan in time. "And we certainly didn't want to go to the CIA, which I suppose knows how to do this sort of thing," Julia said.

She decided to raise the money in Europe. "We went to a number of different countries and got a million here and a million there and then told the Danish foreign minister that we would bring all this money in to the country, but it would only be there for a few days," Julia said. "They put it in a big cash box and put the cash box on a plane that we were using to send some SUVs to Afghanistan. Two people sat in one of the cars, holding the box. Nobody knew, except those two, that there was money in there."

Julia said that as an economy measure—if one can believe there were any in this war—the U.N. ordered a cheap charter flight from Copenhagen that had to refuel in Iran. There, the plane broke down. "Oh my God, we'll never see this money," Julia thought.

The plane was fixed and flew on to Kabul, but it landed at the wrong airport. The pilots had flown to Bagram Air Base, the military airport, instead of the civilian airport, where armored SUVs stood waiting to transfer the box of cash. "They arrived in the middle of the night," Julia said. "They got off the plane, and British officials met them saying, 'What are you doing here?'"

"We're on a secret mission," one of the cash box carriers replied. When he explained that they were carrying U.S. dollars to pay Afghan civil servant salaries, the British officials escorted them to the home of the British High Commissioner, who hid the box under his bed until they could decide how to distribute the money.

The box arrived just in time for Karzai to announce at the international donor conference in Japan that his civil servant salaries would be paid.

"We've been fortunate to assist in the payment of salaries since January, and people have money," Julia told PBS's Ray Suarez in April. "People are starting to be able to buy commodities, buy food, shop. This is all progress."[139]

Over the next two years, Julia used the trust fund to help with various commissions that met in Afghanistan and to set up an international conference center with proper equipment. In June 2002, an emergency *loya jirga*, a traditional Afghan tribal assembly, was convened to form a new transitional government and elect interim leader Karzai as president. Julia's program provided funds to fly representatives to Kabul from each of what were then the nation's 21 provinces. "We used prop planes," said Julia. "I don't know if we had any World War II planes, but we had planes from all over the place. It was the biggest airlift the U.N. ever did. We flew in 1,500 delegates from all over the country to the conference site."

Then she needed a tent large enough to accommodate so many people. But there was no tent to be found in Kabul. Julia's team located one at the Munich *Oktoberfest* and had it flown in. "Isn't this ironic," she said. "You have an *Oktoberfest* tent in an Islamic country that doesn't serve liquor. But it worked perfectly." The tent was set up on the grounds of Kabul Polytechnic University, where for the first time in more than 20 years, the elected representatives debated the election of a new government.[140]

Lesson learned: "What we found was that in post-conflict, there are many humanitarian groups that come in and do wonderful things—immunizations, start-up schools and whatnot," Julia said. "Very few of them do it under the guise of the government. These are special projects. But the UNDP initiatives that we took were so closely aligned to the government's priorities and the peace process that we found that having this kind of trust fund where you could fill in the gaps gave the new authorities in the country the sense that they were in control. They were paying the salaries; they were doing the commissions; they were holding their own voting processes. It was absolutely key to the credibility of the new authority."

Leaning far back in her chair, Julia was reflective: "Now I don't know what's going to ever happen in Afghanistan, with the drugs and the corruption, but at least the first couple of years of the new Afghanistan started with some solid footing, and I was really excited to be a part of that."[141]

Julia retired in 2004 at U.N's mandatory retirement age of 62. She'd grown weary of the commute between Washington and New York on the Delta shuttle, and she was eager to spend more time with Will, who was having his own problems with the administration of George W. Bush.

As chief legal adviser to Colin Powell, Taft took issue with the administration's policy toward people captured in the conflict with al-Qaida. In a series of memos, Justice Department attorney John Yoo argued that Bush was not bound by the Geneva Conventions, which prohibited torture of detainees because, as commander in chief, he had the authority to approve any technique necessary to protect the nation's security.

Taft disagreed. In a memo written on January 11, 2002, he warned that the Justice Department's argument was "seriously flawed" and that such a ruling could wind up endangering U.S. troops. "A decision that the [Geneva] conventions do not apply to the conflict in Afghanistan in which our armed forces are engaged deprives our troops there of any claim to the protection of the conventions in the event they are captured," Taft wrote.

The memo proved highly controversial, and Will was excluded from further involvement in administration's consideration of how to treat detainees. After Bush's re-election, he resigned quietly from the State Department and returned to private practice.

CHAPTER 13

JULIA & THE DALAI LAMA:
A SPIRITUAL JOURNEY

Of all the world leaders and VIPs that Julia met throughout her life, the Dalai Lama was probably her favorite.

Secretary of State Madeleine Albright had appointed Julia to be the State Department's Special Coordinator for Tibetan Issues in January 1999. The position was established as a compromise between Albright and Senator Jesse Helms, chairman of the Senate Foreign Relations Committee. With strong bipartisan support, the Congress had been pressing heavily for the appointment of a special envoy for Tibet, but the State Department objected because of its official "one-China policy." In 1997, they settled on the position, and Julia became the second person to hold it. Her predecessor, Gregory B. Craig, had been moved to the White House to serve as a special counsel to President Clinton during the impeachment proceeding and the post had been left vacant for many months.

Over the years, there had been a dramatic turnaround by U.S. politicians in response to the pleas of the Dalai Lama for greater concern and attention to the needs of the Tibetan people, whose ancient Buddhist country had been ruled by China since 1950. The Tibetan spiritual leader and his government had entered into an agreement on Tibetan self-rule with the Chinese government, but communist aggression against the Tibetans and their ancient traditions made that impossible. In 1959, the Dalai Lama fled Tibet for exile in India after a failed uprising against Chinese rule. While the Dalai Lama has pursued a "Middle Way" policy that seeks "genuine autonomy" for Tibetans within the People's Republic of China, the Chinese government insists that he wants independence or separation and protests any high-level meetings by foreign leaders with him as improper interference with its internal affairs.

To show his concern for Tibet without raising tension with China, President Clinton would occasionally "drop by" meetings that his top administration officials had with the Tibetan spiritual leader. Once he walked down a White House hallway and said "hi" to the Dalai Lama from behind a palm tree before slipping into another meeting. "It was really extraordinary," Julia told me. "Nobody could say that he met with the Dalai Lama, but they could see that there was interest."

Early on in her tenure, Julia was fortunate to meet with the Dalai Lama at the State Department. He briefed her on the plight of the Tibetan people, the status of dialogue between the Tibetans and the Chinese, the important role that Buddhism plays in the Tibetan culture and the issues facing Tibetan refugees. He also extended an invitation to visit Dharamsala, India, his home and seat of the government-in-exile, to meet Tibetans, interview new arrivals and experience Tibetan culture. "The Dalai Lama was thoughtful and sincere, and Julia felt an instant connection with him," said Kate Friedrich, Julia's closest adviser on Tibetan issues at the State Department. "She immediately began laying the groundwork to make the unprecedented trip to India." After a year of planning, in January 2000, Julia was ready to go. Officially, her mission was to assess the status of U.S.-funded humanitarian programs for Tibetans refugees in India.

Julia's trip coincided with the daring escape from Tibet to India of the third-highest-ranking lama in Tibetan Buddhism, the 14-year-old Karmapa Lama. "His trip through the icy passes of the Himalayas was considered a major embarrassment for China," wrote the *New York Times*.[142]

Two hours before Julia was to leave for India, she received a call from a State Department official in New Delhi saying that India objected to her trip, believing it had some connection to the Karmapa Lama's arrival in Dharamsala and that she planned to whisk him off to the United States.

"Stop, who's the Karmapa Lama?" Julia asked, genuinely perplexed.

When the official explained that the Karmapa Lama was one of Tibetan Buddhism's most revered spiritual masters, Julia said that her trip had nothing to do with him, that she only wanted to learn more about the plight of Tibetan refugees. "I've got my visa, and I'm coming," she said.

India was clearly worried about stirring up more tensions with China, which, according to a BBC report on the visit, "had plunged to a new low two years before by India's nuclear tests and statements by the Indian defense minister that China represented the biggest security threat to his country."[143]

Indian officials put tight restrictions on Julia's visit: she could not meet with the Dalai Lama; she could not meet with the Cabinet of the government-in-exile; she could not meet with the Karmapa Lama; and she could not have a news conference. "So I said, 'Yes, sir, anything you suggest will be fine,'" Julia said. "I agreed to their terms."

Accompanied by Kate Friedrich, Julia boarded a flight at Dulles International Airport for New Delhi. The transatlantic voyage took nearly 46 hours, with delays in Europe and flight diversions caused by the "Indian fog," a thick cloud of smog that reduces visibility so much during the winter that planes often cannot land. When they finally reached New Delhi, they were joined by Lodi Gyari, special envoy of the Dalai Lama, and two officials, a State Department colleague from Washington and an embassy control officer.

The next day, they all flew to Northern India. "We were on a small plane with only eight seats, and the trip was fairly turbulent and a bit scary," Kate Friedrich recalled years later. "But Dharamsala is beautiful. Nestled in the foothills of the Himalayas, it's about 4,500 feet above sea level and surrounded by snow-capped mountains. The air is clean, the view is breathtaking, and Tibetan culture thrives there."

When they arrived at the region's small airport and began loading into cars, everyone noticed that each of the vehicles displayed an Indian-issued license plate with the words "Government-in-Exile" written across the top and a bumper sticker that said "Free Tibet." "We wondered how this might be construed by the press, since it's contrary to U.S. policy," Kate said. "But there didn't seem to be any press around, and this was our ride, so we all piled in." Thirty minutes later, upon reaching the summit of Dharamsala, they found mobs of news reporters waiting for them.

"The hype around the arrival of the Karmapa and our coincidental trip seemed to capture the imagination of the masses," Kate said. "As we attempted to take in our official welcome—a traditional snow lion dance performed by members of the Tibetan Institute for Performing Arts—it was nearly impossible to enjoy, with reporters shouting 'Are you here to take the Karmapa to America?' and cameras flashing all around us. Given the circumstances, we thought about whether to write a brief press statement or even just answer their initial questions, but Julia decided that it was best to keep her word and say nothing. So we checked into our respective hotels."

Julia, Kate and Lodi stayed in Kashmir Cottage, the unheated home of the Dalai Lama's deceased mother, a place so cold that at night they were reduced to burning their briefing books and classified cables in the fireplace with a few twigs to keep warm.

"We were there for several days, and the Dalai Lama invited me for tea," Julia told me. "I wrote him a note saying I would not be able to do that, but I would see him in Washington." She also had several requests to meet the Cabinet. Julia decided to bend the rules—a little— by meeting with everyone in the Cabinet but one person, so it could not be considered a full Cabinet meeting! She hosted the group in her bedroom at Kashmir House.

"While the venue was a little unconventional," Kate said, "with men sitting on beds, floors and the ends of tables, she knew that the press would not find out, and it would give her the opportunity to hear directly from the ministers about their concerns."

After a second night of burning briefing materials to keep warm, the team packed up and headed to lower Dharamsala, to visit the Norbulingka Institute, before heading out. Named for the Dalai Lama's summer home, the Norbulingka is an art institute dedicated to teaching young Tibetans traditional sculpture, thangka painting, metallurgy, wood carving and appliqué. The local artisans presented Julia with a traditional thangka painting, which she hung in her office at the State Department and then donated to the Special Coordinator's office, where it hangs today.

Snow began to fall, and the team decided to leave Dharamsala before the route to the airport, with its hairpin turns, unpaved roads and deep ravines, became even more treacherous than usual. When they arrived, they waited 90 minutes for the plane before realizing it had been canceled. "We had only one choice," Kate said: "to drive to the Pathankot train station near the Kashmiri border and try to catch the all-night, 14-hour, mail train to Old Delhi. The snow was really starting to come down, and we only had about an hour to get there." Luckily, they were in the hands of a skilled group of Tibetan monk drivers who delivered them to the station with only a minute to spare. "The train started moving as soon as we got on," Kate said.

Once on board, they learned that the private cabins were sold out, and they were relegated to the coach section. After settling in, their State Department colleague asked if anyone had heard what he just heard. "We quieted down to listen," Kate said. "Four children were coughing."

"That's a TB cough!" the official declared. "Everybody move!" Luckily for them, Lodi Gyari had enough pull with the conductor to secure a private cabin to finish the journey.

They arrived in Old Delhi the next day and prepared to make their way through one of the busiest train stations in the world. The embassy control officer said he had only one instruction for them: "If anyone tries to take your luggage, just let him have it!" Julia and Kate thought he was kidding, but he wasn't. After navigating through a virtual sea of people and managing to hold on to their belongings, they arrived at the American Embassy, where a staffer informed them that India's foreign secretary would like to see Julia before she left India later that day.

"Apparently, the Indian press had released wild stories about Julia making arrangements to take the Karmapa to the United States," Kate said. "Of course, she went to see him immediately. The two had a good conversation, and Julia made her way to the airport to leave for Bhutan."

Despite the chaos, Julia called the whole experience "magical." Her trip would mark the first time a U.S. Special Coordinator for Tibetan Issues had visited the region, and that alone—even without a meeting with the Dalai Lama—was a clear signal to the Tibetans that the United States would be a friend.

Julia flew from India to Bhutan to meet with its king, Jigme Singye Wangchuck, the fourth Dragon King, who grilled her on how the Karmapa had escaped and where he was staying. The king also told Julia that his son, the crown prince, was a student in the United States at Wheaton College and wanted to transfer to Georgetown University. "Oh, my daughter, Julie, transferred to Georgetown," Julia replied. "She will show him around." And Julie did!

Julia had touched all the bases. By treating each of the principals with respect—agreeing to restrictions, attending formal dinners, enjoying the local cultures, flying to Bhutan to meet with its king and doing him a personal favor—and generally networking within the Buddhist community as only Julia knew how—she succeeded in gaining more support around the world for Tibetans and the plight of the refugees. "It was really important how some of these little connections actually work," she said. "Of all of the diaspora groups that I have worked with in my career, the Tibetans are the purest. They are absolutely focused; they will rally together, and the Dalai Lama is well served. But he has also made every effort possible to come and spend time here and support them.

"The effort now is to the get the Chinese to have a dialogue, which will result in the Dalai Lama being able to go back and do a pilgrimage. Many of us hope this will happen before the [2008 Beijing] Olympics. We believe that the one vehicle for ensuring there won't be a separatist movement is the Dalai Lama, because people will listen to him. They listen to whatever he says. It is hoped that China will comply and accept him back for a pilgrimage, but they're taking a very tough line right now."

Over the years, Julia saw the Dalai Lama often. In October 2007, two years after she began battling cancer, she met with him again. He was in Washington to accept the Congressional Gold Medal, and on the afternoon of the ceremony, he invited Julia to meet privately with him in his suite at the Park Hyatt Hotel. The spiritual leader wanted to know how his old friend was doing.

Julia, again in chemotherapy, was self-conscious about her thinning hair and cursed herself for not wearing her new wig. She confessed to the Dalai Lama that she was getting weaker, and he prescribed a Tibetan medicine.

"It's a pain reliever and an immune booster and a spiritual booster," His Holiness said.

"It sounds like that's exactly what I need," Julia replied. "But you're the best boost I have right now. I feel very serene."

"Are you hurting?" the Dalai Lama asked.

"No," she said. "I'm tired."

DL: "Are they going to cure you?"

JVT: "No. They said that there's no cure."

"You need to do two things," the Dalai Lama told Julia. "Follow the instructions of your doctors to the letter and find time for your own contemplation and tranquil time to meditate."

"Well, I've done the former," Julia replied, "but I'm not very good about meditating. I'm not a Buddhist."

"You don't need to be a Buddhist," the Dalai Lama said. "I tell people who want to convert to Buddhism not to do it, that they ought to be whatever their religion is, just be good at that religion. You don't have to convert."

Before parting, Julia told the Dalai Lama that although her health was frail, she would do anything she could to help him. "I don't know how much time I've got," she said, "but whatever time I have, I would be glad to do any special assignments for you, anything in the world because in the last decade, this has been one of the most rewarding aspects of my life, being involved and supporting you."

The Dalai Lama started to thank Julia, but she hadn't finished. She had one more question: "Are you making any efforts to try to help the Muslim faith accept or express in a more positive way some of the elements of Islam, which are not unlike some of the elements of Buddhism: the compassion, the reaching out to family, the caring business. Have you done anything, or do you plan to do anything? Because I think you might be the one of the few people who could bridge this divide."

The Dalai Lama told Julia that he had met with a number of Muslims in India and San Francisco and that he thought there was an opportunity for dialogue, but there was no structure in place for him to do that.

"Well, we have all of these discussions," Julia replied, "and all of the euphoria over the gold medal has put the spotlight on Tibet, but many of us think that this is far beyond Tibet, that this is really about the way societies need to heal each other and live within the diversity of the planet."

The Dalai Lama asked Julia if she knew any Muslims. "Well, my godson turned Muslim on me," she replied, "and now he's a professor at the University of Washington, and he is a very, very devout Muslim, who's committed to trying to find a middle way. My daughter-in-law and all of her Turkish relatives are Muslim, and they are very moderate, conciliatory and progressive. So there are people and groups to work with. I don't know how much energy I have, but if there is any way I can be helpful, just let me know."

Julia had been scheduled to spend five minutes with the Dalai Lama, and their meeting lasted almost a half hour. Later that same day, Julia and I sat in her backyard in Washington, and she told me about the exchange. "I think that one of the aspects of him which is so empowering is that he is not trying to inflict his ideas or his religion on people," she said. "He just believes you have these answers inside yourself, and you live with them, and you do the best you can."

Five months later, on Saturday morning, March 15, 2008, Julia died at her home in Washington, surrounded by her family. Several days earlier, Ken Bacon and her friend Sheppie Abramowitz had gone to see her with reassurance that they would coordinate with other relief agencies to bring more pressure on the White House and Congress to protect displaced Iraqis.[144] "She was stretched out on the sofa, but we didn't realize how sick she was," Sheppie said. "She was all business. She wanted to know exactly what we were planning to do."[145]

Julia fought for the rights of refugees until almost her last breath. And in large measure, it was this spirit, this determination, this creative energy that continues to burn and keep her flame alive.

In October, the Dalai Lama celebrated Julia's life at a private luncheon in Washington and posthumously awarded her the International Campaign for Tibet's Light of Truth Award, which honors those who contribute to the public understanding of Tibet and fight for human rights. His Holiness spoke in soft tones about Julia's dedication to the world's refugees and mentioned the arduous trip she made to Dharamsala. Will Taft accepted the honor in his wife's name. A highlight for Julie and Christof was that the Dalai Lama took their hands, held them to each other's hearts and blessed their marriage.

Julia would have loved it all—the honor for her dedication to the issues of refugees and human rights from a man she so deeply admired, the ceremony, the presence of so many of those closest to her heart. And the Dalai Lama was right. She had the answers inside herself and lived with them and did the best she could.

ACKNOWLEDGMENTS

Writing about a friend is a challenge. I loved Julia Taft as much as I admired her. And I love her family, which is now intertwined with mine. Julia brought me into her circle of friends, and they are now my friends. To put it simply: I hope I got her right!

I would particularly like to thank Julia's husband, William H. Taft IV, and their children, Maria, William and Julie, who opened their hearts and troves of special memories, not easy when the grieving process is still fresh. And I thank the Aquarians and their husbands for sharing stories about Julia as a young woman: Sue and Jim Woolsey, Margie Axtell and Russ Stevenson, Jacqueline and Frank Samuel, Bobbie and Bill Kilberg, Margot Humphrey and Louise Tucker.

Patricia Goldman and Stephen Kurzman, longtime friends of Julia and Will, described Julia's earliest days in Washington. Ann and Marshall Turner dusted off countless files from their White House Fellows years. Will Taft's goddaughter, Kate Adams (née Brown), sent delightful family stories, and Julia's godson, Jack Brown, reconstructed Will's elegant father-of-the-bride toast at Julie and Christof's wedding. Judy Harkness Taft's graciousness and understanding as I went forward with this project made every family request easier.

Many of Julia's colleagues contributed anecdotes and reviewed chapters, offering significant help with historical detail and perspective. I owe a large debt of gratitude to Sheppie Abramowitz, Renee Bafalis, Elizabeth Becker, Jim Bishop, Wesley Clark, Chester A. Crocker, Kate Friedrich, William Garvelink, Christopher R. Hill, Robert V. Keeley,

Suzanne Kindervatter, Timothy Knight, Fred Krimgold, Carolyn M. Long, Mary Beth Markey, Bill Nash, Lionel Rosenblatt and Strobe Talbott.

Two longtime friends, who first encouraged me to write about Julia, didn't live to see the final product. We lost Brooke Shearer and Ken Bacon, also to cancer, not long after Julia, and also much too soon. Their energy and spirit live on in the people and projects they inspired, including this one.

My sister, Carolyn Jacoby, was interested in every aspect of Julia's life and listened patiently, as she has for so many years. My friends Viveca Novak, Linda Lipsett, Merna Guttentag and Ann Van Dusen read chapters and held my hand. Once again, Margaret Dalton kept me walking.

Copy editor Marcia Kramer was a stickler for detail with a sharp eye and a broad understanding of the issues. Jane Karker, president of Maine Authors Publishing, with David Allen and Cheryl McKeary, have guided me into a new world of book publishing. Ria Biley doublechecked us all.

Henry Putzel Jr. was a dear close friend of Will Taft's parents for more than half a century and has been enthusiastic about this project from the start. As always, I relied on Uncle Henry to be my final proofreader.

With great appreciation, I thank my dearest ones for their love and support: Leila and Ben Fitzpatrick, who, with their magnificent twins, Abigail and Emma, bring magic and laughter to our lives; and Julie and Christof, whose dedication to the downtrodden made Julia's heart sing— and mine as well. For Christof, a special thank you for asking me to write Julia's story and for pushing me to finish the manuscript whenever I got discouraged.

And finally, my husband, Mike, the love of my life for 40 years, has been at my side every minute, offering encouragement, advice and perspective, day by day, month by month, chapter by chapter. This book is also for him.

ENDNOTES

1   Hevesi, Dennis. "Julia Taft, Official Who Led Relief Efforts, Is Dead at 65." *New York Times*. March 18, 2008.

2   Clark, Wesley K. Interview with AB. April 13, 2011.

3   Bacon, Ken. Eulogy for Julia. March 24, 2008.

4   Bacon, Ken. Interview with AB. June 10, 2008.

5   Ibid.

6   Bafalis, Renee. Interview with AB. July 9, 2008.

7   Taft, Julia. "Fleeing Our Responsibility." *Washington Post*. June 24, 2007. Op-ed page.

8   Vadala, Shirley. Letter to Julia Taft. Undated.

9   Ibid.

10 Taft, Julia. Interview with AB. June 14, 2007.

11 Ibid.

12 Taft, Julia. Interview with AB. June 14, 2007.

13 Ibid.

14 Taft, Julia. Interview with AB. Library of Congress (LOC) oral history. Her discussion of events in my interview is almost identical with her oral history.

15 LOC oral history.

16 Taft , Julia. Interview with AB. June 14, 2007.

17 Taft, Julie. White House Fellows resume. LOC oral history.

18 LOC oral history.

19 Taft, Julia. White House Fellows resume.

20 Drake, Hudson. Telephone interview with AB. March 6, 2011.

21 Gannon, Frank. White House Fellows program exit interview. November 16,

1972. Nixon Presidential Library and Museum. http://www.nixonlibrary.gov/forresearchers/find/textual/central/smof/gannon.php

22   Goldman, Pat. Interview with AB. March 1, 2011.

23   Turner, Ann. Interview with AB. April 15, 2011.

24   "At War with War." *TIME*. May 18, 1970.

25   White House Fellows handbook, 1971-72.

26   http://www.senate.gov/artandhistory/history/common/generic/VP_Spiro_Agnew.htm

27   LOC oral history.

28   Ibid.

29   Associated Press, January 6, 1971. Interview with AB.

30   Turner, Marshall. E-mail to AB. April 15, 2011. Richard Nixon Presidential Library & Museum. President's Daily Diary.

31   Taft, Julia. Interview with AB. June 14, 2007.

32   Turner, Marshall. E-mail to AB. April 4, 2011.

33   Taft, Julia. Interview with AB. June 14, 2007.

34   Kurzman, Stephen. Interview with AB. March 10, 2011.

35   Samuel, Frank. Interview with AB. April 18, 2011.

36   Kurzman, Stephen. E-mail to AB. May 10, 2011.

37   Taft, Julia. LOC oral history.

38   Samuel, Jacqueline. E-mails to AB. May 8 and May 10, 2011.

39   Samuel, Frank. Interview with AB. April 18, 2011.

40   Tucker, Patricia. *Money*. July 1973. Pp.35-40.

41   Samuel, Jacqueline. Interview with AB. April 18, 2011.

42   Martin, Allison. "The Legacy of Operation Babylift." http://www.adoptvietnam.org/adoption/babylift.htm

43   Taft, Julia. Interview with AB. June 7, 2007.

44   Thompson, Larry Clinton. *Refugee Workers in the Indochina Exodus, 1975-1982.* P77.

45   Taft, Julia. Interview with AB. June 14, 2007.

46   Taft, Julia. LOC oral history.

47   "Women Power," *People,* July 21, 1975. P.60.

48   Keeley, Robert V. E-mail to AB. May 12, 2011.

49   Taft, Julia. Interview with AB. July 27, 2007.

50   The breakdown Taft gave adds up to more than the total 134,505 refugees in the system.

51   Binder, David. *New York Times.* June 9, 1975, P.1.

52   Le, Minh. Interview with AB. September 10, 2011.

53   Keeley, Robert V. Eulogy for Julia. March 24, 2008.

54   Rosenblatt, Lionel. E-mail to AB. April 25, 2011.

55   Samuel, Jacqueline. E-mail to AB. December 20008.

56   Axtell, Margie. E-mail to AB. January 18, 2011.

57   Humphrey, Margot. E-mail to AB. May 24, 2011.

58   Woolsey, Sue. Interview with AB. March 30, 2011.

59   Axtell, Margie. E-mail to AB. January 19, 2011.

60   Tucker, Louise. E-mail to AB. May 23, 2011.

61   Taft, Julie. Interview with AB. January 16, 2011.

62   Woolsey, Sue. E-mail to AB. January 15, 2011.

63   Taft, Julie. E-mail to AB. May 8, 2011.

64   Taft, William H. V. E-mail to AB. June 3, 2011.

65   Woolsey, Sue. Eulogy for Julia Taft. March 24, 2008.

66   Full disclosure: Julia Taft invited me to be a member of Aquarius two years before she died.

67   Hershey, Robert D. Jr., "Aiding Disaster Victims; Small Agency Helps a Great Power Lighten Human Suffering." *New York Times.* September 13, 1988.

68   Taft, Julia. Interview with AB. June 17, 2007.

69   Crocker, Chester. E-mail to AB. April 11, 2011.

70   LOC oral history.

71   Taft, Julia. Interview with AB. October 17, 2007.

72   Garvelink, William. All information from him supplied by e-mail to AB. April 4, 2011.

73   Associated Press. March 25, 1989.

74   Leland, Mickey. "What African-Americans Can Do about Starvation in Africa." *Ebony.* August 28, 1989. Pp.81-82.

75   Taft, Julia. ABC's "Nightline." Interview with Ted Koppel. December 1988.

76   Blackman, Ann. Interview with AB. June 14, 2007.

77   Hevesi, Dennis. *New York Times.* March 18, 2008.

78   Anderson, Dr. Gail. Atlanta Journal-Constitution, January 27, 1989. P.1E.

79   Anderson, Dr. Gail. Atlanta Journal-Constitution, January 27, 1989. 1E; Davidson, Oliver: USAID After-action report on Armenia. Situation Report #6. February 12, 1988. P.3.

80   Garvelink, William. Email to AB. April 4, 2011.

81   Bacon, Ken. Eulogy for Julia Taft. March 24, 2008.

82   Bafalis, Renee. Interview with AB. July 9, 2008.

83   Garvelink, William. E-mail to AB. April 4, 2011.

84   Davidson, Oliver: USAID After-action report on Armenia. Situation report #10. December 15, 1988. P.1-4.

85   Taft, Julia. ABC's "Nightline." Interview with Ted Koppel. December 1987.

86   Blackman, Ann. *TIME* file from Taft's December 15, 1987 news conference in Moscow.

87   Anderson, Gail. *Atlanta Journal-Constitution*, P.1E.

88   Anderson, Gail. *Atlanta Journal-Constitution*, 1E; Davidson, Oliver: USAID After-action report on Armenia. Situation Report #6. February 12, 1988. P.3.

89   Taft, Julia. Interview with AB. July 10, 2007.

90   Bafalis, Renee. Interview with AB. July 9, 2008.

91   Taft, Julia. Interview with AB. July 10, 2007.

92   Goldman, Ari L. "U.S. Team Calls Scale of Quake Unimaginable." *New York Times*. December 23, 1988.

93   Taft, Julia. ABC's "Nightline." Interview with Ted Koppel. December 1987.

94   Krimgold, Fred. Interview with AB. June 26, 2008.

95   "How Gorbachev Views the Cold War's End." *TIME*. December 19, 1988. P.18.

96   Bafalis, Renee. Interview with AB. July 9, 2008.

97   Goldman, Ari L. "U.S. Team Calls Scale of Quake Unimaginable." *New York Times*. December 23, 1988.

98   Krimgold, Fred. Interview with AB. June 26, 2008.

99   Taft, Julia. "MacNeil/Lehrer NewsHour" interview. December 1987.

100   Taft, Julia. Interview with AB. July 10, 2007.

101   Ibid.

102   Krimgold, Fred. Interview with AB. June 26, 2008.

103   Ibid.

104   Bafalis, Renee. Interview with AB. July 9, 2008.

105   Ibid.

106   Blackman, Ann. *TIME* file from Taft's December 15, 1987 news conference in Moscow.

107   NBC's "Today." December 16, 1988.

108   Blackman, Ann. *TIME* file from Taft's December 15, 1988 news conference in Moscow.

109   Sudetic, Chuck. "Shelling by Serbs in Bosnia Intensifies," *New York Times*. April 7, 1992.

110 Darnton, John. "Croats Rush Work on Crumbling Dam," *New York Times*. January 28, 1993.

111 Rosenblatt, Lionel. Refugees International World Bridge blog. September 29, 2009. Interview with AB. March 15, 2011.

112 Rosenblatt, Lionel. Interview with AB. March 15, 2011.

113 Knight, Tim. E-mail to AB. April 21, 2011.

114 Bacon, Ken. Eulogy for Julia. March 24, 2008.

115 Carroll, Rory. "US Chose to Ignore Rwandan Genocide," *The Guardian*. March 31, 2004.

116 Bonner, Raymond. *New York Times*. December 18, 1994.

117 Bishop, Jim. Interview with AB. April 22, 2011.

118 Long, Carolyn M. Interview with AB. April 14, 2011.

119 Bishop, Jim. Interview with AB. April 22, 2011.

120 Kindervatter, Suzanne. Interview with AB. April 14, 2011.

121 Kindervatter, Suzanne. E-mail to AB. May 11, 2011.

122 Tyler, Patrick E. *New York Times*. September 6, 1995. P.1

123 Taft, Julie. E-mail to AB. March 28, 2011.

124 Taft, Julia. Interview with AB. June 10, 2007.

125 Perlez, Jane. "U.S. Weighs Using Food as Support for Sudan Rebels." *New York Times*. September 21, 1998.

126 Krieger, Heike, editor. *The Kosovo Conflict and International Law: An Analytical Documentation*, 1974-1999. P.104.

127 Perlez, Jane. "NATO Stance Is Said to Hurt Both Alliance and Kosovo." *New York Times*. September 21, 1998. P. A4.

128 Clark, Wesley K. Interview with AB. April 13, 2011.

129 *Washington Post*. Editorial. September 16, 1998. P.A16.

130 Erlanger, Steven. "Russia Vows to Push Arms Pact, to Pave Way for Summit," *New York Times*. March 8, 1998, P.A11.

131 Smith, R. Jeffrey. "Kosovo Refugees Find Cold Comfort in Montenegro." *Washington Post*. December 8, 1998. P.A33

132 Landler, Mark. "Obama's Choice: To Intervene or Not in Libya," *New York Times*. March 5, 2011. Week in Review. P.1.

133 LOC oral history.

134 Talbott, Strobe. E-mail to AB. February 3, 2011.

135 The information on Taft's trip to Macedonia with Talbott and Ambassador Christopher Hill has been pieced together from AB's interview with Julia Taft on June16, 2007, and interviews with Talbott on April 25, 2011, and Hill on May 6, 2011.

136 Taft, Julia. Interview with AB. June 16, 2007.

137 Confidential source.

138 Malloch-Brown, Mark. Email to AB. September 18, 2011.

139 Suarez, Ray. PBS "The MacNeil/Lehrer NewsHour." April 18, 2002.

140 http://www.nytimes.com/keyword/loya-jirga?scp=1&sq=2002%20loya%20
jerga%20in%20%20Afghanistan&st=cse.

141 Taft, Julia. Interview with AB. June 16, 2007.

142 Yardley, Jim. "Tibetan Lama Faces Scrutiny and Suspicion in India." *New York Times*. February 7, 2011. P.1.

143 "Diplomatic Jitters over Lama's Visit." BBC News. January 10, 2000.

144 Bacon, Ken. Eulogy for Julia Taft. March 24, 2008.

145 Abramowitz, Sheppie. Interview with AB. June 4, 2011.

ABOUT THE BOOK

OFF TO SAVE THE WORLD: How Julia Taft Made A Difference is the story of one of the United States' top humanitarian relief experts who, over three decades, became a legend in her field.

Starting in 1975 when she was 32 years old, Julia Taft directed the task force that managed the resettlement of refugees from Vietnam, Laos and Cambodia. Over the years, she essentially invented the way the United States government responds to natural and man-made disasters around the world, demanding basic rights for those whose lives are turned upside down by civil war, famine, religious persecution, earthquakes, floods and insect infestations.

Based on interviews in the year before she died, as well as on conversations with her friends and colleagues, author/journalist Ann Blackman describes some of Taft's most important humanitarian missions: her direction of the American relief effort during the Armenian earthquake, Operation Lifeline Sudan, the Siege of Sarajevo, the crisis in Kosovo and her trip to Afghanistan in 2001, when she worked for the United Nations.

Taft also discussed her fascinating and enduring friendship with the Dalai Lama, whom she met in 1999 when she was the State Department's coordinator for Tibetan issues. When she was battling cancer, Taft had a personal conversation with His Holiness, and he offered her advice: meditate.

Woven together, the interviews, a Library of Congress oral history, and dozens of newspaper stories about her over the years, paint a mosaic of a witty, determined, hard-charging and idealistic woman who not only ran some of the most dramatic relief efforts of her generation but also influenced the debate at home and abroad as the international spotlight moved from Vietnam, Cambodia and Laos to the collapse of the Soviet Union to ethnic conflicts in Africa and the former Yugoslavia. Taft's personal story also reflects the history of three decades of political unrest and social upheaval in the 20th century, at home and abroad.

There are funny stories and poignant ones, heroic moments and terrifying ones. At Julia Taft's request, this book is dedicated not only to her children, but also to her friends in the field, who continue the unsung work that captured her heart.